Wedding Style

F O R   T H E   U N I Q U E   B R I D E

Wedding Style

FOR THE UNIQUE BRIDE

♥

RITA WILLIAMSON

foulsham

LONDON • NEW YORK • TORONTO • SYDNEY

For Mark, my husband and partner

In memory of Etty, who never minded the mess

ISBN 0-572-01745-6

Copyright © 1994 Rita Williamson

Phototypeset in Great Britain by Typesetting Solutions, Slough, Berks.
Printed in Slovakia

Contents

Preface

I believe that there should be sentiment in every wedding: in the dress, the flowers, and even in the choice of guests. It should all reflect your little loves and fancies, your superstitions and your family customs. Every wedding should be special and every wedding should be different.

It is my hope that this book will show how a little imagination, a little care and attention to detail and perhaps a little boldness can make your wedding enjoyable, beautiful and unique.

But how can one book help each reader to become a unique bride when every idea in it will be read and used by all its other readers? Will these brides not simply be carbon copies of each other?

No, because this book is designed to encourage young brides, mature brides, second-time-around brides, all brides, to use their *own* ideas. If ten different women read this book, then ten different brides with ten different ideas, styles and skills will organise and plan ten very different weddings. With this book, I want to encourage all brides to try for a look or style that is special and unique to themselves.

For an inveterate spendthrift I adopt a curiously parsimonious attitude when it comes to weddings, and wedding dresses in particular, so my readers can be assured that I am not about to lead them off down long, expensive blind alleys. Why should you sacrifice the wedding of your dreams for the sake of a price tag when originality and imagination can bridge the gap? This book will give you, your mother, or your friends the confidence and courage to bring your dream within your grasp.

Use creativity to make your wedding unique. No other dress will have the same embroidery as yours, or use the colours you have chosen. No other dress will use lace from your grandmother's gown, or have the love and attention in every stitch that only you can give it.

For the purists who recoil at the short-cuts I suggest, I offer no defence but this: the wedding ceremony, and all the pomp and circumstance associated with it, has only one purpose – to celebrate the marriage of two people. It is not necessary to spend a fortune on vastly expensive items; and if the finished item is something you are justifiably proud of does it matter if you cut a corner or took a short-cut?

Those with a high degree of skill and artistry can go ahead and work to their limits of excellence. Those with basic or limited skills can go at a slower pace and with more modest goals. Perhaps the finished result may not be as expert as something from the hands of a professional, but it will be a triumph of your skills, care and imagination, and all the more special for the effort that went into it.

I want you to *enjoy* your wedding day. I have tried to combine snippets of advice, good ideas and experience into a book that will help you plan a wedding that demonstrates your own unique style, a wedding that is fun, personal to you and, ultimately, a special event to celebrate a most special occasion.

Photograph Acknowledgements

Berkertex Ltd 10, 63, 67, 77, 78 (bottom), 86.
Brian Betts 172.
BOC Ltd 27.
Mrs Jackie Butler 73 (left).
Mrs Sue Davies 15 (bottom).
Fantastic Fireworks Ltd 166.
The Food and Photography Company 19, 23, 62, 78 (top), 87, 94 (top), 103, 107, 110, 111, 115 (left), 118, 119 (bottom), 121 (top), 122 (left), 126 (left, bottom right), 127, 147 (top), 155, 158 (top right), 163 (bottom), 165, 169.
Heli-flair (Andrew Mardell) 158 (top left).
Mrs Denise MacArthur 119 (top).
Mr & Mrs C. Moore 13 (top), 162 (top).
The Old Blacksmith's Shop, Gretna Green 14.
Mrs Gladys Oliver 98, 130.
Randall Williams Photography (Chris Titmus) 94 (bottom), 121 (bottom).
Vogue/Butterick Co. Ltd 58, 59, 69, 70, 75 (right).
John M. Walker 2, 122 (right), 131 (bottom), 174.
Mrs Carolyn Wardrop-White 75 (left).
Mrs Anne Watkins 16.
Mrs Joan Williamson 12, 13.
Mark Williamson 6, 15 (top), 30, 31, 35, 38, 39, 51, 53, 54, 71, 72, 73 (right), 74, 80, 81, 82, 83, 85, 90, 91, 102, 115 (right), 126 (top right), 131 (top), 138, 147 (bottom), 158 (bottom), 161, 163 (top), 171.
Rita Williamson 45, 76, 151, 156, 159.

Acknowledgements

Writing a book, however isolated and lonely it may seem at times, is not something anyone can really do by themselves. This book has been no exception and I am grateful to the people who have helped me so willingly and so faithfully during the preparation of this manuscript.

Very special thanks must go to my husband, Mark, for his enlightening comments and constructive editing. I particularly appreciated his patience and artistry in photographing various items to illustrate this book.

I would like to offer special thanks to professional photographers Jeff and Cally Rand who have been more than generous with their help. I would also like to thank Karen Hutchinson for being so brave as to model for me.

So many companies and individuals have been kind to me while I was preparing this book that there are simply too many to name here, so I have taken the liberty of listing them all separately a little later on. I am delighted to give you full details of these most helpful organisations.

People who must be thanked over and above all others are the many brides and grooms included here –without them this book would be awfully dull!

The Brides

I am grateful to the many brides and couples pictured in this book who gave their permission for use of their photographs. These include:

Mr & Mrs A. Barrett, Mr & Mrs Biggley, Jackie & Howerd Butler, Mr & Mrs Dahdra, Mr & Mrs Davies, Judith Dodd, Jane Dodd, Mr & Mrs Dover, Mr & Mrs Fidgeon, Mrs Marjorie Fry, Mr & Mrs Harris, Alan & Karen Hutchinson, Mr & Mrs Hyde, Mr & Mrs Kempson, Denise McArthur, Mr & Mrs McIver, Ruby and Cyril Moore, Mr & Mrs Neave, John & Gladys Oliver, Mr & Mrs Padduick, Mr & Mrs Perkins, Mr & Mrs Ralph, Mr & Mrs Redfern, Mr & Mrs Simmonds, Mr & Mrs Turner, Mr & Mrs Wadsworth, Mr & Mrs Warran, Mr & Mrs Warwick, Mr & Mrs Waters, Mrs Jean Watkins, Mr & Mrs Wheeler.

I am indebted to Joan and Tom Williamson for their permission to use the delightful old family photographs reproduced at the beginning of this book.

Chapter 1
Taking the Deadlock out of Wedlock

'People think that I can teach them style. What stuff it all is!
Have something to say and say it as clearly as you can.
That is the only secret of style.'
MATHEW ARNOLD

Finding your Style

How does one pick a style for a wedding? Isn't the question of style already laid down in tablets of stone? Aren't all weddings sombre affairs with girls in white dresses and men in dark suits?

The answers to that are: no, no, a thousand times NO! A wedding is the culmination of a courtship and the start of a new life together. It is, above all things, a celebration. It is about you and your partner's personal thoughts on marriage. It is about the things you will continue to share. All of these aspects should be reflected in the style of your wedding, along with love, romance and joy.

Look at the collection of photographs that show weddings which have taken place over the last century. They each capture the perfect image of a bride of that time, yet each bride was special in her own way. Each of them has a story to tell which makes their wedding different from any other. Their choice of gown, of flowers and friends made their wedding day individual to them.

The basic style of your wedding will depend on your personal circumstances, the strengths of your beliefs about marriage and togetherness and, of course, your own personalities. If you are outgoing, socially-minded people you will opt for a style of wedding that reflects this. You may want a fairly informal church wedding followed by a rousing party-to-end-all-parties. But if you are quiet, shy people you may prefer a discrete register office wedding attended by your closest friends, followed by a small celebration in a fine restaurant before making your way off to your secluded honeymoon spot.

You may even consider having your wedding in a distant or exotic location. Yes, this is quite possible. There are several tour companies that offer complete wedding packages, including full wedding arrangements and a fantastic honeymoon. Unfortunately you can't marry just anywhere in the world, only in those countries where the marriage is recognised by English law. If the thought of a marriage in Disneyland or on some tropical beach thrills you, or the prospect of making your vows in the wilderness of the bush excites you, why not look into this.

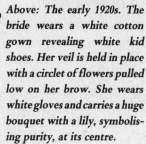

Above: The early 1920s. The bride wears a white cotton gown revealing white kid shoes. Her veil is held in place with a circlet of flowers pulled low on her brow. She wears white gloves and carries a huge bouquet with a lily, symbolising purity, at its centre.

Right: 1924. This bride does not wear white, but a new dress which will be worn as 'best' after the wedding. Note that hemlines have crept up, but not for the older ladies. The two bridesmaids wear pleated dresses and carry flowers. Instead of floral headdresses they wear matching hats. Notice how much fur is worn.

Above: 1931. Hemlines have risen dramatically now! The matron of honour and the bride wear the latest cloche hats. Bouquets and posies are fresh flowers gathered from the garden. I was intrigued to see that the matron of honour's shoes would not be out of place in a 1993 shoe shop.

1935. Here is a perfect example of a bride who adheres to my philosophy of a 'unique bride'. Ruby wears a dress of white silk which she made herself and a headdress and veil that was borrowed from someone in the family. She also wears her mother's wedding shoes which had been saved for 40 years for the purpose. The bridesmaids' dresses were also made by Ruby and were in shades of pink, lilac and blue organdi. The little hats, which are trimmed with lace and ribbon, were copied from a photograph Ruby saw in a magazine. The flowers were freshly-cut chrysanthemums from her father's garden.

Below: 1938. How similar this bride is to Ruby. Even the bridesmaids wear similar little caps. How we all adhere to fashion...

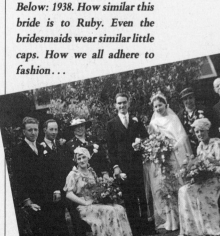

Above: A wedding of the 1940s. The men are in uniform, which reflects the time of war, and the bride wears a suit, because of the difficulty in obtaining new clothes and fabric. I particularly like the little veil attached to her hat.

Alternatively if the appeal of watering-holes and mosquitos is not high, then why not opt for a plain civil ceremony and expend your romantic and creative energies on the reception or honeymoon? The young couple pictured below opted for a civil ceremony and then travelled to Gretna Green to pay an affectionate tribute to their Scottish roots with a 'marriage' over the anvil at the Old Blacksmith's Shop.

Not until you have decided on the basic style of your wedding can you think about all the many other aspects of a wedding that have to be planned, booked and organised. Firstly, you must find a style that is *you*. The obvious starting point must be to decide how you and your groom want your day to be and how *you* want to look. If there is an image in your mind of how you've always imagined yourself as a bride – whether it's milk-maid sweet or Mae West – go for it.

However, don't be surprised if you find yourself changing your mind. I know a couple who decided, for reasons of economy, to marry at a register office. The bride intended to wear a smart suit or day dress, and the couple planned to round off the day with a small party at her father's house. As the planning progressed, they realised that, in their heart of hearts, they wanted a bright and jolly celebration. Plans were changed. They still married at the register office, but the bride wore full bridal regalia, they had two delightful children as attendants and finished off the day with a lavish party for all their friends. It was, they decided, a once-in-a-lifetime occasion and not something they should hold back on.

So, think carefully and find a style that you are comfortable with: it may be formal, simple, spiritual or wildly extravagant. Then consider how to reflect this in the many aspects of your wedding.

Perhaps the best place to start is to decide how you wish to look. Find a dress that suits you perfectly; one that makes you feel good about yourself. Go to as many bridal shops as you can and try on dresses you fancy. Go into the shops and try them on, don't just look. And don't stop until you find the one that flatters you and makes you feel 'right'; like a bride.

Don't be timid, try everything and, most important, be open to suggestion. Ask your groom what he thinks you should wear. He may surprise you! Don't forget that he may be holding a dream of how his bride should look. I knew one bride who had an easy time choosing a dress; she only looked at off-the-shoulder styles because her groom said that's how he saw her as a bride.

Above: A bride of the 1980s whose bridesmaids echo the return of romanticism generated by the Princess of Wales, which continued throughout the rest of the decade. Here the bride wears an ivory cotton gown which had been handed down through the family, whilst the bridesmaids wear ivory satin in traditional styles trimmed with royal blue. The bride and the matron of honour carry simple sheafs of flowers.

Right: 1967. This Scout master marries the Guide mistress and their day is made all the more special by a 'scouting' guard of honour. In line with the fashion of the time the bride wears a tiara with her hair piled high in curls. Her gown is a white, A-line brocade, and she carries a bouquet of russet and gold flowers: true Brownie colours.

Listen to the advice of the sales staff; they've dressed hundreds and thousands of brides and know what they are talking about. If they offer you advice, at least think about it. If you are sure you want a white dress, try on a cream one anyway. You may be surprised by how much more flattering it is to your colouring.

Even if you are convinced that you should wear only a short dress or a suit, try on the whole works: long dress, train, veil and tiara, just in case. You may find a whole new bride lurking inside you! Then again, you may just prove that you do look best in a two-piece suit. Have an open mind, try several options and ultimately you will be sure that you have made the right decision.

If looking around the shops does not help you to identify the sort of dress you want, or if you are lucky enough to look absolutely gorgeous in all of them and just can't make up your mind, then you are in that wonderful position of being able to become a truly 'unique bride'. You can adopt any style of dress you wish from traditional, through unusual and on to the downright weird!

But how to begin?

Consider the illustration below left which shows Brian and Anne Watkins who married in 1957. He was the local Scout master and she was the Cub mistress. Their day was made that much more special by the attendance of the entire local Scout troop. Ten years later, another Brownie mistress married John Davies, another Scout master. You can see in the illustration on page 15 that their links with the Scout movement certainly made an impression on their day. Sue even used gold and tawny Brownie colours in her bouquet! How different these weddings were to any others that occurred on the same days. They were, in short, unique. Both couples took hold of an idea or subject that was dear to them and included it in their celebrations. They shared their day with people they cared for, and who cared for them.

Of course, just because you work for British Telecom doesn't mean you have to have a BT guard of honour or hold the reception in a phone box. But one would, for example, expect at least one telemessage from your friends and colleagues!

Adopting a Theme

Why not consider adopting a theme to run through your wedding to give you something to plan around? It can be something very personal to you

1957. The Scout master and the Cub mistress marry to the obvious delight of the entire guard of honour! The bride wears a tiara and short veil and a waisted brocade gown.

and your groom, as in the weddings described previously, or it could be something as simple as a colour. There are many themes and ideas you can use to give a structure or core to your wedding plans.

Perhaps you could use a geographical location, a type of culture, a period of history, a sport, or a type of music as a theme. Have a competition with your groom or family to see who can think of the most inventive ways of using your chosen theme. Look at colour supplements, magazines, books or go to the library for inspiration. Then, when you have a *huge* list, you can pick those ideas you fancy and those that are practical. What about using the following topics as themes for a wedding? Chinese, Spanish, military, Mexican, wildlife, Hollywood,

Below: If there is a gypsy in your soul, let her out and wear a gown of white flounces made startling with flamboyant embroidery in primary colours. Carry wild flowers rather than cultivated blooms.

Below right: Hint at the un-restrained passion of the hot-blooded Spanish with a dress inspired by the flamenco. Let the lush froth of petticoats contradict the modest look of a lace mantilla and ornate comb.

Left: Go Japanese and wear a kimono-style, lace and satin gown with a detachable train. What an exotic negligée this could become!

futuristic, rock and roll, Alice in Wonderland, royalty, opera, movies, ballet – the list is virtually endless. But don't forget, it doesn't have to be obvious, just something that pleases you. And don't simply copy what you find; stamp your own individuality on it. You may want a Hollywood look to your wedding, but there must be more of you in it than Greta Garbo!

Having prompted you to explore extravagant themes, it may be as well to point out now that you should take care not to be too outrageous and do something you may later regret. I know of one mother who threw out her wedding photographs in a fit of shame when her grown-up children fell about laughing at the fashions. Personally I would have thrown the children out! But the point is clear. Current fashions are just that, current. In ten years' time you may wish you'd been a little more conservative. In fifteen years time a 'bold gesture' may just look foolish.

The style of your wedding will, of course, depend on funds and your fancy, but the secret of how to make it unique and special is: try not to do the obvious. Let a style suggest itself and remember that you are not obliged to spend a fortune.

Not everyone will notice each little item that enforces your theme; indeed perhaps it should be sufficiently subtle to be almost invisible. But you will know how structured everything is and how much thought has gone into it all. Of course, the entire wedding doesn't have to hang on your every whim. Just use it where you think it works best.

Let me use my own wedding as an example of what I mean. My husband's business is space technology; my preferred reading matter is science fiction. We met in Florida, USA, at the first launch of the Space Shuttle in 1981. You will not, perhaps, be too surprised to learn that we decided to include some aspects of space in our wedding. We chose to do it with music: while we were in the vestry signing the register, our guests listened to 'Jupiter, Bringer of Jollity' from *The Planets Suite* OP.32 by Holst. Apart from enjoying the notion of 'jollity' and the fact that the piece contains the tune of a favourite hymn, another reason for choosing 'Jupiter' was that I heard it on the radio the morning after my husband's romantic, midnight proposal! Later, at the reception, we gave the first dance to 'The Blue Danube' by Strauss. Aficionados of the SF movie classic *2001: A Space Odyssey* will know it was part of the film score. The space connections weren't obvious and we didn't bother to explain our choices, but they made the day personal to us.

You may think some of this is far-fetched and that it would be too obvious to have a theme running through everything. But at all weddings the same old themes and little traditions keep cropping up: horseshoes, sweeps, black cats. So why not choose your own theme? It can be done without being tasteless and it can be achieved either with great expense or on a miniscule budget. Let's take one theme in greater detail.

The Country Diary of an Edwardian Lady
Groan . . . yes it's a theme that has been 'done to death' and is on everything from bedsheets to oven gloves. But it will give you ideas as to what can be done with a theme, and the fact that it is everywhere can work in your favour as you will find endless sources of material in high-street shops. Buy the book or borrow it.

- Find country-diary stationery in the shops and hand-write the invitations in brown ink on cream paper.

- Buy larger country-diary cards (blank inside) and get a quick-print photocopy shop to print inserts for the the Orders of Service in brown ink on cream paper.

- Buy serviettes and tablecloths for the reception. If you can't get tablecloths, use country-diary wallpaper!

- Hand-write menus and place cards to go on the tables. Quote some of the little verses from the book at the top of each card.

- Request country-diary linen or kitchenware on your wedding list.

- Choose an Edwardian-style dress for you and a tail coat and winged collar for the groom.

- Dress the bridesmaids in Edwardian-style frocks with pantaloons, or copy the dark velvet dress and lace collar that Edith Holden wears on the back of the book.

- Have your bridesmaids carry hoops of flowers and let the pageboys wheel hoops and sticks (if you dare).

- When is the wedding? Use Elizabeth Holden's illustrations for that month for inspiration.

- Carry a posy of the flowers and plants described for your chosen month.

- Find the right perfume – honeysuckle, lily of the valley, rose – wear it or give it as gifts.

When to Marry

The time of year is a very important factor in any wedding, and highlighting the month or the season could lend an immediate and subtle theme to your wedding. Be an autumn bride and fill the church with, or dress your attendants in, the

Blast away the chill of autumn with this bold combination of navy and startling coral. The suit is of brocade and looks like seventeenth-century quilting.

The autumn theme is continued and exploited to magnificent effect in this wonderful cake with its stunning and original decoration.

wonderful and glorious shades of fall; vivid golds and burnished coppers will add warmth and excitement to the spectacle.

A spring bride will have a vastly different day. She can fill the church and hall with the bright, primary colours of spring flowers and arrange to have the photographs taken in the local park, which will be awash with golden yellow daffodils and deep blue hyacinths.

When had *you* considered marrying?

A friend of mine set the date of her wedding to coincide with the lily of the valley blooming in her mother's garden. Her mother and grand-mother had carried blooms from the same stock in their bridal bouquets, and it was a small family tradition in which she wanted to share.

Another girl I know chose a summer wedding so she could carry the pink roses from a bush in her father's garden. The bush was planted when she was born and her father cut blooms from it every year for her birthday.

If you love the crisp starkness of winter, consider a winter wedding. It will make your wedding dramatically different to that of a June bride. You and your attendants can enter the church in rich robes of velvet. You can wear a huge fur-trimmed cloak, or a fantastic costume straight from the Snow Queen and dazzle them all with the icy shine of 'diamonds'. Don't serve your guests sherry at the reception, warm their hands with hot mulled wine. Be different.

But that's just the season, the actual day you choose could also have a bearing; a mid-week wedding will be quite different to a weekend wedding. Mind you, when considering the day of your marriage you might like to bear the following rhyme in mind:

Monday for wealth
Tuesday for health
Wednesday the best day of all.
Thursday for losses,
Friday for crosses
And Saturday, no luck at all.

It seems that most modern brides are damned!

Where to Marry

Of course, a lot will depend on where you will marry. It could have a bearing on the style you decide upon. For example, you live in a typical old English village and the church is just a walk away from your parents' house. The reception is going to be tea in a marquee on the village green. What could be nicer than the Edwardian 'anyone for croquet' look? All the ladies can languish in white lace as they sip lemonade and nibble daintily at strawberries and cream. The men complete the picture in blazers and slacks or even cricketing whites.

Alternatively, you are marrying at the local register office on a busy high street in the middle of town and the reception is at a posh local pub with a disco. A flapper dress with a softly draped veil and a circlet of white freesias will look elegant at the civil ceremony, whilst the same dress under the disco lights will flash with the brilliance of 5,000 sequins.

But we have to remember that the dress need not be the focal point of the wedding. There are other hooks to hang your ideas on, other ways to introduce a style or a theme.

Favourite Things

If the when of your wedding really doesn't matter, if you have no choice about it, or you simply cannot get excited by the thought of spring as a theme, consider other things. What makes you happy? What little things hold special memories for you and your groom?

Whether it's raindrops on roses or whiskers on kittens, including a few of your favourite things can make your wedding unique. Some people may raise their eyebrows at an unusual style of wedding but, as long as it is in good taste, you should do whatever pleases you. Measure things by your pleasure, not the expectations of fashion and the opinions of others. Have a whale of a time to celebrate *your* wedding.

Just one or two of your, or your groom's, 'favourite things' can suggest a theme or style for the wedding and stamp your personality on the entire event. Other brides may choose roses or the colour blue, but not for the same reasons you have. Your reasons are unique so your wedding becomes special to you.

Your Favourite Colour

Whether your favourite colour is green, blue, pink or orange . . . go for it. But remember, if it doesn't suit you, don't wear it, just carry it.

The last three brides in my family have all carried flame-coloured flowers ranging from orange through yellow and peach to cream. Not subtle, but bright and cheery. For my own wedding I, too, decided to carry flame colours and put my bridesmaid in white with the brightest orange silk pinafore I could find. Personally I'm not keen on white sashes on white dresses on pale blonde children. But that is my choice and you will have your own ideas.

Colours also have superstitions attached to them and many of these properties are particularly associated with wedding gowns. If you simply can't choose a colour, the list on page 22 may help you.

There is also this little ditty to think about.

Married in white, you've chosen right
Married in black, you will wish yourself back
Married in red, you will wish yourself dead
Married in green, ashamed to be seen
Married in grey, you will go far away
Married in blue, love ever true
Married in pearl, you will live in a whirl
Married in yellow, ashamed of your fellow
Married in pink, your fortunes will sink.

Which is all fairly depressing if you don't wish to wear white!

Actually the whole notion of marrying in white is relatively modern (compared with how long

Colour Associations

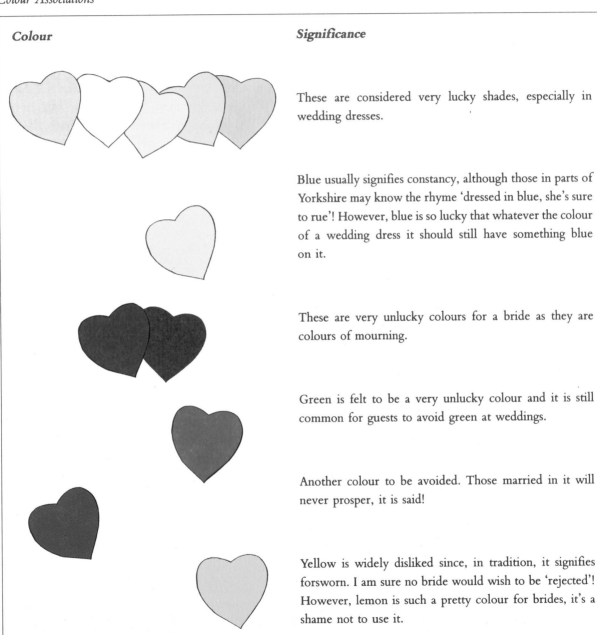

Colour	Significance
	These are considered very lucky shades, especially in wedding dresses.
	Blue usually signifies constancy, although those in parts of Yorkshire may know the rhyme 'dressed in blue, she's sure to rue'! However, blue is so lucky that whatever the colour of a wedding dress it should still have something blue on it.
	These are very unlucky colours for a bride as they are colours of mourning.
	Green is felt to be a very unlucky colour and it is still common for guests to avoid green at weddings.
	Another colour to be avoided. Those married in it will never prosper, it is said!
	Yellow is widely disliked since, in tradition, it signifies forsworn. I am sure no bride would wish to be 'rejected'! However, lemon is such a pretty colour for brides, it's a shame not to use it.

marriage has been around), dating back only as far as Victorian times. Prior to this only the luckiest of brides were fortunate enough to have a new dress, and that was usually in a dark or serviceable colour. Only the rich married in pale-coloured gowns that could be disposed of when they grew dirty or stained. Even then, the notion of white dresses was rare and not taken up until one of Queen Victoria's daughters married in white and set an immediate and long-lasting fashion.

A different culture where red and not white is the traditional colour for marriage. Whatever colour you choose, there is nothing quite as beautiful as a bride – except perhaps the groom!

Around the world, other colours prevail. In China and other Asian countries red is the colour of weddings. During their revolution, American brides chose to wear red as a symbol of freedom. It's funny to think that when the punk era was flourishing in the 1980s, many young brides opted for black or red lace gowns and felt themselves to be totally outrageous. But it had all been done before and their anarchic gestures were simply copies of a much earlier fashion!

Your Favourite Jewels

Had I not chosen to follow my family's little tradition of flame colours, I would have chosen green as my colour theme despite its unlucky connotations. Why? Because my birthstone is emerald, and so is my engagement ring. For me and all others born in May, the emerald is said to be very lucky. One book on superstitions I have says: 'emerald, giving success in love'. What more could I ask?

Interestingly, your fiancé's birthstone is thought to be especially lucky in an engagement ring, so that's two choices of stone for your ring.

In case you don't know what your birthstone is, or hadn't realised that precious stones have meanings or properties attributed to them, I have included a list of stones associated with particular months of birth. It is not a complete list of all precious stones and you may find that different reference sources give slightly different lists, but that's good because you can pick and choose even more!

There are many items specifically associated with star signs or signs of the zodiac, and often

Birthstones

Month of Birth	Stone and its Properties
January	The garnet, which signifies truth and constancy.
February	The amethyst, which denotes sincerity and has the power of preventing drunkenness in those who wear it (a useful gift for the best man, perhaps!).
March	The bloodstone, which brings courage and presence of mind to its possessor.
April	The diamond, a symbol of innocence and light.
May	The emerald, giving success in love.
June	The agate, or sometimes the pearl. The agate gives health and long life, heals fevers, draws out the venom of bites and strengthens the sight! Surely a must for all brides! The pearl stands for purity and also for tears.

Birthstones

Month of Birth	Stone and its Properties
July	The carnelian or the ruby. Carnelians give a contented mind and, if worn in a silver ring, ensure many friends for the wearer. The ruby has even greater virtues: it gives courage, prevents impure thoughts, preserves chastity and kills reptiles!
August	The sardonyx, a kind of onyx that ensures married happiness.
September	The sapphire, one of Jupiter's stones, has many and varied magical properties.
October	The opal. This stone, although it signifies hope, is often considered unlucky, except for the October-born.
November	The topaz, symbol of fidelity, protects the wearer from the effects of poison.
December	The turquoise, which brings prosperity and prevents quarrels between marriage partners.

they are thought to be very lucky. I have included a chart in Chapter 8 which is worth looking through to find things that are said to be lucky for you.

This is all very well, but how can you use a birthstone? Well, how about using its colour as your theme and then giving the appropriate birthstone pendant as a gift to your bridesmaids, or buying fake birthstones from a DIY jewellery catalogue and studding them over your headdress. Consider its magical properties: look for suitable quotes about love, honesty, chastity or courage and include them as readings, decorations for the invitations, or as useful snippets in the dreaded speeches.

Your Favourite Flowers

Of course, another favourite topic is flowers. Everyone has a favourite flower. But don't limit yourself to using its colour or simply having that sort of flower in your bouquet or in the church.

You can use them in many ways. Adopt the whole style and shape of the flower; use its scent, its colour and its foliage. Let's look at roses as an example.

You can embroider them on your gown, carry them, have rose buttonholes, put roses on the cake, decorate the invitations with roses instead of horseshoes. Give gifts of rose oils to the bridesmaids, carry a pomander of rose pot pourri, adorn your dress with silk roses, wear them in your hair, wear rose scent, drink rosé wine!

My illustrations shows some of these. Take the idea as far as you can (short of changing your name to Rose!) and you will have the basis of a good wedding theme.

Still stumped for themes and ideas? Okay, let's list half a dozen more and see where they take us.

Cats

Have cat illustrations on stationery, carry catkins and pussy willow, embroider paw prints in white on your dress, give the bridesmaids gifts of toy kittens, let them carry toy cats instead of flowers. Carry a black cat with a colour-themed bow for good luck. Use patchwork somewhere – many traditional patchwork patterns are named after

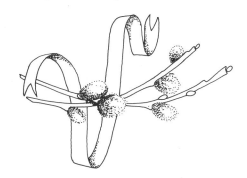

cats: 'puss in boots', 'cat's cradle'. Carry or embroider daisies, as they are known as 'cat posy' in some parts of the country.

Did you know that if the household cat sneezes near a bride on her wedding morning, she will have a happy married life? No, I am not suggesting you pepper the cat, but it may make an interesting snippet in the speeches!

Trains

Perhaps your groom is a steam train fanatic (or do I mean enthusiast?). Why not use the livery colours of his favourite line or train as a theme? Queen Victoria and the railways came of age together so a Victorian dress is a good starting point. Alternatively you could wear a dress suitable for the *Orient Express* or the *Brighton Belle*. Put your pageboy in a guard's uniform and let him carry green flags and a whistle (on second thoughts, forget the whistle!). Let the smallest pageboy or bridesmaid pull along a wooden train

filled with flowers. Have your cake in the shape of a train or embroider trains on the ring cushion. Get married in York or have your honeymoon there so your groom can spend some time at the National Railway Museum.

Balloons

Use ordinary air-filled balloons to jolly up the dance hall or helium-filled balloons to obtain amazing effects such as arches or create entire ceilings of balloons. Mix balloons with expensive or exotic flowers to pad out the floral displays and reduce the expense. You can arrange balloons into the shapes of animals, people or anything that reflects your theme. Make rainbows from balloons or use them as table decorations, pillars, screens, gifts or messages. Overprint them with your names and the date or outrageous messages. Decorate your parents' house and garden to show the entire street you are celebrating (but watch out for rose thorns!). Or strike a more sentimental note and release a cloud of white balloons in lieu of doves, just as you leave the church. Have a balloon 'seller' handing them out at the lych gate. Hire a bouncy castle for the kids to play on, or have a hot-air balloon tethered at the reception; give in to the romance of it all and go for a flight.

You may be able to find details of local balloon suppliers, but it's probably best to contact someone like BOC Limited (see page 189) who have set up a Balloon Hotline and can direct callers to local suppliers, printers and even party decorators. They also supply party packs and organise the delivery and collection of the cylinders of balloon gas if you intend to stage your own spectacle.

Rainbows

Buy stationery printed with rainbows. Have seven bridesmaids and dress each one in a different colour of the rainbow – red, orange, yellow, green, blue, indigo and violet. Carry rainbow flowers, reproducing the colours in all their glory or in pastel versions. Use the seven colours in embroidery on your gown. Embroider rainbows, appliqué rainbows, paint rainbows! Have seven rainbow-coloured ribbons decorating your hair or your gown. Have a rainbow-shaped cake and a

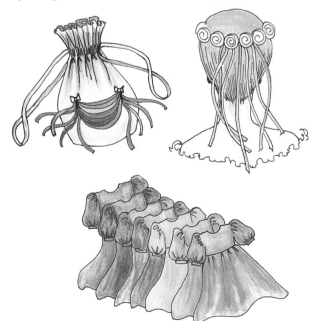

curved bouquet. Decorate the reception hall with crêpe paper swathes of rainbow colours and play music from *Finnegan's Rainbow*.

I particularly like these lines from Christina Rossetti (1830-1894) and you may like to use them in the invitations or let your groom quote them in his speech:

A Birthday

'My heart is like a singing bird
Whose nest is in a watered shoot;
My heart is like an apple-tree
Whose boughs are bent with thickest fruit;
My heart is like a rainbow shell
That paddles in a halcyon sea;
My heart is gladder than all these
Because my love is come to me.'

Carnival

This is a more abstract idea and shows, I think, how a theme can run through a whole event but not be too specific. Bring the excitement and fun of the carnival or circus to your wedding: don't just have a party, have a mardi gras!

Wear a ballerina gown and pretend you're the circus lady that rides on the back of white horses. Dress the attendants in little clown outfits – the sort with coloured pom-poms on white suits. Have a Pierrot and Pierette. Give everyone party hats and masks at the reception, but don't call it a reception, call it a masked ball. Have it in a marquee or tent and get the best man togged up in a red coat and tails to act as master of ceremonies or ringmaster. *Everyone* should be given party hats and streamers!

Snow

If you are having a winter wedding, why not use snow or snowflakes as your emblem? As you know, snowflakes have six sides or points, so the number six can figure large at your wedding. Have a six-sided cake with snowflake decorations. Have six guests to each table at the reception. Use stylised snowflakes on the stationery. Have doilies everywhere at the reception. Machine embroider snowflakes in white on your dress (this is so simple anyone can do it, so no excuses!). Carry masses of gypsophila to look like snow. Let the bridesmaids carry baskets of rice or rice paper dots as confetti to look like snow. Wear white velvet, fur or feather trim. At the reception, play every song you can think of with snow in the title (there's snow business like show business!). Serve vanilla ice-cream snowballs and sugar-frosted fruit.

Chapter 2
Stitches in Time

'Although a Queen, yet she her days did pass
In working with the needle curiously.'
JOHN TAYLOR

Surely there is no more special garment or gift than the one that has been hand-made or crafted especially for you. By using your own creativity, or by asking friends to offer their skills, you can introduce true originality to your wedding. Incorporate a traditional or favourite skill in your wedding and be a bride unlike any other.

This chapter does not intend to teach you how to use the traditional skills discussed; instead it attempts to show you that craft skills can be exciting and add an extra dimension to the style of your wedding. Choosing roses as your theme is fine, but having roses as a theme and embroidering them yourself is something else, something unique.

The bride who contributes her own artistic skills to her wedding must certainly be classed as a bride with style. Such skills could be anything from using your own dress design, making the bridesmaids' dresses, to arranging your own flowers or drawing a picture for the invitations. Here we are going to look at eight common yet traditional needlecraft skills and consider how they can be used to give your wedding that special touch. These skills are: embroidery, beading, appliqué, quilting, patchwork, smocking, crochet and knitting.

Of course, this chapter cannot include the whole range of crafts and skills open to you. There are other equally beautiful skills that I do not mean to ignore, but I imagine that any woman who can make her own lace or make her own silk flowers will not need me to give her ideas! Here I describe how to use the more popular skills, for which all one needs are the correct tools, a clean pair of hands, some peace and quiet and somewhere to work.

Chapter 8 contains patterns and diagrams which can be used with many of these skills, along with simple tips and instructions that are common to most of them.

In the following pages I shall, of course, talk about the wedding dress and attendants' outfits, but don't be fooled into thinking that they are the limits. Whilst you certainly can't crochet the Order of Service sheets, you can crochet lace for your dress, lace for the bridesmaids' dresses, lacy surrounds for the bridesmaids' posies, or small coasters for the wedding party to keep. You can even use your christening shawl (the one Grandma crocheted) as a fancy cloth for the cake table. Think stylish and original. Be unique.

Think how pleased you'll be when you hear your guests chatting among themselves saying, 'Did you see that lovely hand-made . . . such a clever idea . . . must have taken her ages . . . takes after her mother with her hands . . . I've never seen anything like it . . .' You'll need no more proof that you have succeeded in being a unique bride.

Below: Embroidering roses around the neckline of this plain silk bridesmaid's dress gives it an individual touch.

Right: Outline and infilled versions of the rose motif on page 21 add style with the simplest of techniques.

Beading along the edge of a piece of cloth gives it weight, movement and interest. Here *it also emphasises the lovely contrast in fabric textures.*

Embroidery

Embroidery is not as popular as it once was. At one time it was an unusual young lady who could not embroider a sampler or make and decorate her own gown. Indeed it was considered a necessity. In the eighteenth century, Lady Mary Montagu wrote:

'I think it as scandalous for a woman not to know how to use a needle as for a man not to know how to use a sword.'

Like swordsmanship, needlecraft is no longer a requirement for the 1990s. Indeed we can buy such gorgeous fabrics we have little need to make them more lovely. But there is no doubt that embroidery is a fascinating and satisfying pastime and one which, if you have the skills, you can use to make your wedding unique.

Embroidery doesn't have to be all daisies on doilies or cross stitch on canvas. It can be white silk on the front of your wedding dress or red roses on the bridesmaids' dresses. Then again why not take the palest pink or blue and scatter embroidered lovers' knots all over your dress? Embroidery can be used as the starting point to create a whole new dress, or can simply reinforce your chosen theme.

The best thing about embroidery is that it does not require very specialised tools. In fact you probably already have most of them in your sewing box.

You can use almost any yarn that takes your fancy, from sewing-machine thread to embroidery cottons, but for the beginner I would suggest that ready-bought skeins of embroidery thread will give you a quality look whilst being easy to handle. Moreover, there are hundreds of colours from which to choose.

One way really to personalise your gown is to embroider a design of your entwined initials, making it into a perfectly unique and beautiful dress. This is the sort of personalisation we are aiming for here. Your initials can be used to create a monogram, to be used by itself or repeated to form a simple pattern. Alternatively, you can sew one single monogram and encircle it with a garland of daisies and french knots and put it slap-bang over your heart! Then again, why not personalise the ring cushion in this way?

Just think how unique your bridesmaids will be if you embroider their initials on each of the dresses. Think also how simple it is: a plain dress with one single piece of embroidery on the bodice yoke. Of course, if your attendants are called Susan, Samantha and Sally, you may think twice about this, but the theory is good.

Look at your dress design and see where embroidery could be used. The style of your dress will tell you where you can't embroider, so take your pick from what is left. Obvious places are: neckline, cuffs, hem, collar and waistband. You may also be able to concentrate your efforts on the front bodice panel, the back bodice panel or the hem of your train.

If you have chosen a theme or adopted a motif for the whole wedding, echo it in your embroidery. If you are carrying roses, sew them on your dress; if you are Scottish, sew little thistles.

a

b

c

d

Your initial plus that of your groom becomes a monogram (a). Embroider it once or repeat it until it makes its own pattern (b). Alternatively, use it alone with the tiniest embellishment of a daisy or two (c), or surround it with a garland of daisies and knots and sew it over your heart (d)!

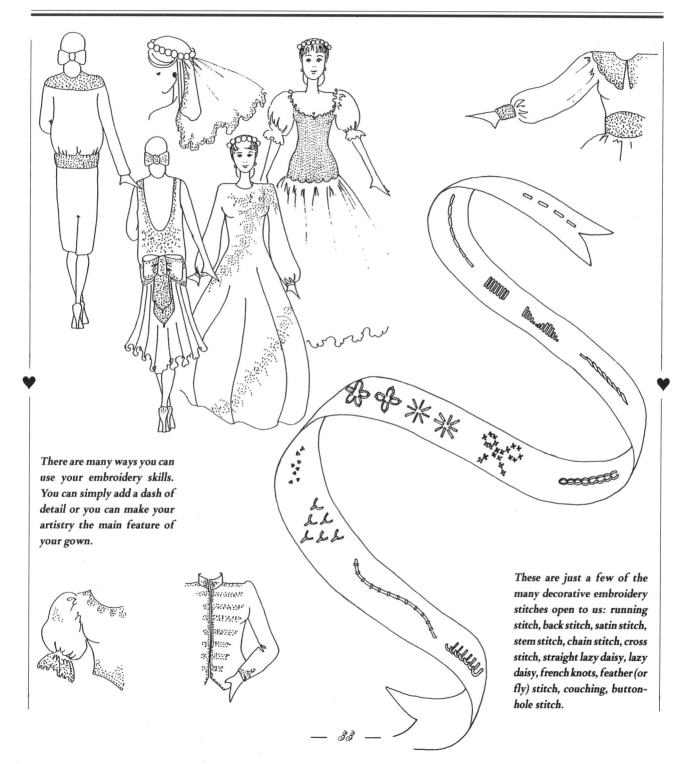

There are many ways you can use your embroidery skills. You can simply add a dash of detail or you can make your artistry the main feature of your gown.

These are just a few of the many decorative embroidery stitches open to us: running stitch, back stitch, satin stitch, stem stitch, chain stitch, cross stitch, straight lazy daisy, lazy daisy, french knots, feather (or fly) stitch, couching, buttonhole stitch.

Turn a budget, shop-bought dress into something special by embroidering rich roses around the neck. Embroider over lace to make it look like truly expensive Swiss lace and not the 40p-a-metre stuff from the local market.

There are a number of different stitches to use in embroidery and I have illustrated perhaps the most well known. Just looking at the shape and style of some of the stitches can give you ideas. Probably the simplest are the straight daisy and lazy daisy stitches. Like real daisies, they are simple and common, but gather a few together and you have a posy; use a cluster of daisies around another more exotic flower and you have a bouquet. The very same is true when you embroider with them.

You could make the embroidery on your gown the main feature of the dress or indeed of the entire wedding. If one embroidered the illustrated fantasy flowers in bright, primary colours with jewel-bright greens for foliage, your fabric would be like a gypsy shawl. How easy it would then be to introduce gypsy aspects into your wedding. Dress your bridesmaids in gaily coloured skirts with white peasant blouses and let them carry 'tambourines' of flowers with ribbon streamers. Exchange the traditional carnation buttonholes for sprigs of white heather. If you can't manage to hire a gypsy violinist to entertain you, why not organise some real country dancing?

However, if you embroidered the same flowers in muted shades of old rose with dusty blues and greens, you would capture the essence of seventeenth-century embroidery or crewel work and would find that you might want to echo the style in your dress and accessories. You could wear

Above: Fantasy flowers. Embroider any or all of them in gypsy flamboyance or Elizabethan subtlety.

Opposite: A beautiful ring cushion, ideal as a lasting keepsake.

a Tudor or Elizabethan-style dress complete with ruffs. The front panel of your dress would, of course, boast your prized embroidery and details of it would be echoed on your gloves and shoes. Your bridesmaids would wear plain gowns with white aprons and bonnets with touches of matching embroidery. They would carry small posies or tussie mussies.

But you don't have to embroider clothes. Why not embroider, in the palest colours, a tablecloth for the top table or the cake stand. Let it be justifiably admired on the day then keep it as an heirloom and use it for anniversary dinners. Alternatively you could turn it into a duvet cover and use it on your marriage bed.

Use your skills with a needle to provide flowers out of season. Embroider exotic lilies erupting from the pocket on your bridesmaid's pinafore or stitch a garland of flowers on the tablecloth.

There are endless ways of using embroidery. You can decorate hand-made gifts such as little purses to hold the bridesmaids' gifts. On your pageboy's dungarees, you can embroider a spray of flowers erupting from his pocket. If you are feeling bold you can embroider a whole bouquet on the bridesmaid's pinafore.

But be realistic about what you want to do. If you are not very sure or very good at embroidery, choose simple patterns and attempt only small designs. Sew posies rather than bouquets. There is no doubt that if sewing is hard for you, the fact that you have done any will make your dress, and indeed your whole wedding, that much more special.

Beading

Beadwork has been used as ornamentation from the earliest times. One has only to think of Cleopatra's jewelled collars to realise that the ancients had the better of us. Beads have been used the world over by primitives and stylists alike. So although I would not suggest you trim your wedding gown with a sharks-tooth fringe, or a cowry-shell motif, I do suggest that you bead it. Why not consider an Egyptian-style dress?

Jewelled gowns are no longer the province of the Royals, the rich, or Italian dress designers. Beading has recently become popular in wedding dresses and more and more gowns, virtually encrusted with jewels, are coming into reasonable price ranges.

Check out the wedding shops and you'll find them full of dresses weighted down with beads –

and beautiful with it. Gowns like these can make you feel like a queen. If the gown you buy is loaded with jewels or dripping with pearls, echo the style with some hand-beading on the bridesmaids' dresses. Alternatively, it may be that the style of dress you buy is plain and you feel it needs cheering up. Beadwork instead of plain embroidery will transform it. Remember, if the shop assistant says those dreadful words: 'This is one of our more popular styles...' you will instantly want to do something to it to make it individual. Beading is a good place to start.

Whilst not wishing to undermine the skill or artistry of the adept bead-worker, I think that beading is well within the grasp of a beginner. If you can sew on a button, you can do beadwork. Indeed, buttons themselves should be seriously considered as items of decoration.

If you have a good imagination and feel confident that you can sew beads, be daring and create your own designs from which to work. Use beads for their size, shape, texture and colour. Let the beads suggest a pattern to you. Be bold.

If you are not as confident, a simple way to start is to embroider and bead a piece of trimming as in the examples of Jackie's and Ruth's dresses (pages 73-4). Use a piece of lace as a guide and enhance the natural pattern of it with well-placed sequins and pearls. This can be added to the dress, or whatever you are making, later.

Remember, beads needn't be fastened down tight – allow some of them to move. Use crystal droplets or swinging pearls around edges to create fringes. Let the beads move and your gown will shimmer and twinkle with a life of its own as you glide up the aisle.

There are several suppliers of special beads, indeed whole shops devoted to the product, but chain stores, craft shops and even small haberdashers sell a wide selection of beads which are more than enough for the beginner. You will, I am sure, be amazed and intrigued by the range available. The photograph on page 38 shows a piece of

Make beading the main feature of your bridal outfit by copying the bejewelled elegance of the Pharaohs. The jewelled collar is really a cloak and underneath it you can wear a simple white gown. Gold chains and strings of beads falling from a headband or cap will complete the Egyptian image.

Left: Here we see how the patterns in lace motifs are enhanced with beads and sequins on Jackie's dress.

Below: This freestyle bead-work shows just some of the sorts of beads available for bridal wear.

Above: Ruth's dress. Here we have lace enhanced with a few pearls and bows. Note the iron-on diamante and pre-bought bows sewn over bows patterned in the lace.

Right: Six bead edges to decorate veils, hems, etc.

freestyle beadwork which uses just a part of the range of one supplier.

Most people think of pearls as white round beads, and sequins as brightly coloured 'fish scales' that you find on a ballroom dancer's dress. Both thoughts are wrong and very out of date. Pearls don't need to be white and they certainly needn't be round. These days they can be obtained in soft colours and a variety of shapes. Sequins come in just about every colour, shape and size under the sun.

You will see in the example of the embroidery on Jackie's dress (far left) that we used several bead types and experimented with colour. I particularly enjoyed decorating this dress, as the warm cream satin allowed me to use gold beads. The resultant embroidery was like nothing we had seen in the shops and the bride loved it for its originality.

There are several ways to sew on beads and I have described the most common in the illustration overleaf. No doubt when you get a bead catalogue, you will find lots of other more interesting beads and will find a way of using them.

Beads don't have to be sewn on – glue can be equally effective. You will see from the example

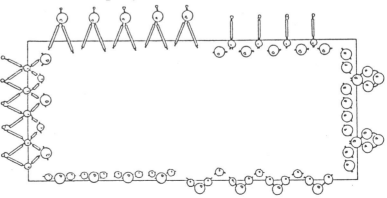

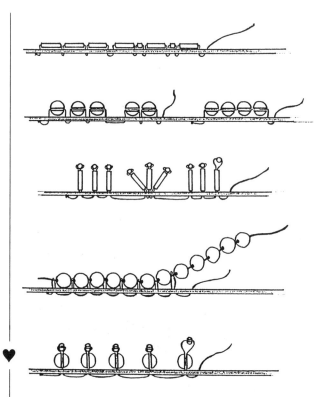

Methods of sewing beads to fabric

of Ruth's dress that there are several round diamante with no visible means of support – they are glued on. What's more, they have even survived a turn through the washing machine! You can also buy whole motifs of iron-on diamante and, for the woman who is short of time, they may be just the thing to add a little something to a plain dress or jacket.

Beading is better suited to some dresses than to others. A flapper dress can be encrusted with beads and fringes of beads without being odd, and a Tudor-style dress just cries out for clusters of jewels. A gown made of chiffon, however, could

be pulled out of shape by the weight of too many beads.

You don't have to copy a historical style to use beads: modern dresses also lend themselves to the technique. Turn a plain department store dress into a jewelled, designer-style cocktail dress by adding sequin motifs as epaulettes, or splashing the front with dazzling jewels.

Shoes, too, can be transformed by beads. Turn plain white satin courts into Cinderella's slippers by beading the shoe or adding jewelled shoe clips.

You can also make a white satin or velvet cover for your Bible and bead a suitable motif on the front. If you prefer (and it's less work) make wide, beaded, ribbon tongues and trail them from the Bible.

Bead your hat or Juliet cap. Hats and head-dresses are the very best place to have moving beads. Ensure that some beads hang loosely. Every time you move your head these will twinkle and shimmer. If you're one of those people who 'speak with their hands' then beading your gloves is a must. Make your gloves so magnificent that it's a positive delight for your audience to watch you wave your hands about!

Exchange your watchstrap for ribbon and bead that. Carry a bag dripping with jewels and ensure that the ring cushion is an heirloom of beadwork.

Beading along the edge of a piece of cloth is an excellent way to give it weight and movement, so think of where you might use that to advantage. The hem of a dress, the edge of a cloak or shawl, or even the edge of your veil could be treated in this way. Beware of overdoing it though: a smack in the face from an over-beaded veil could be painful!

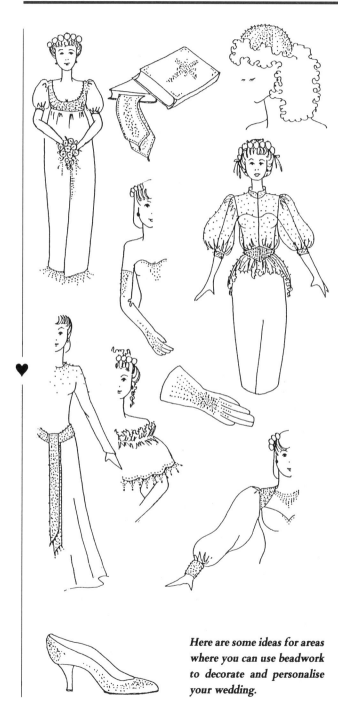

Here are some ideas for areas where you can use beadwork to decorate and personalise your wedding.

Appliqué

Appliqué is a simple needlecraft technique whereby you stitch pieces of fabric on to a background cloth to form a design. If, as a child, you ever enjoyed cutting out paper shapes and making pictures with them, then appliqué is right up your street. In appliqué, the art lies in the arrangement of the pieces and the skill lies in the manner of fastening them down.

Appliqué may be considered a little unusual for a wedding dress, but then we are looking for the unusual here. Don't think of appliqué as simply cutting out shapes and sewing them on to another piece of cloth in a pattern. Instead, think of it as a method of joining together several different layers of fabric to get interesting and beautiful effects.

For perfect appliqué you can either turn under the edges of your shapes and fasten them with invisible stitches, or oversew the edges in neat or decorative embroidery. Use whatever method you find easier. But remember to use fabrics of similar weight where possible and preferably ones which do not fray. Materials that are flimsy or tend to fray can be controlled by ironing them to lightweight iron-on interfacing before you cut them. Also, keep the grains of the pieces running in the same direction as the grain of the backing cloth and you will prevent problems with the fabric puckering.

What you appliqué is entirely up to you, and it is here that you can have fun. You can, of course, appliqué simple horseshoes or bows all over the hem of your dress. But why not appliqué great swathes of rich lace in exciting swirls down the bodice and on the skirt?

Appliqué, like all the other skills mentioned here, has a variety of uses.

Think about colour and texture in your appliqué. You can appliqué white satin on white satin and still make it exciting, but you can also apply textured white fabric on to white satin and get a whole new effect. Don't forget the reverse is good too: white satin laid on to knitted or jersey fabrics looks sumptuous. Yet how different it will look if you overlay a colour on to your plain white dress.

Remember also you don't have to appliqué the material flat, or sew down all the edges. Attach only one edge and you have a frill or flounce, attach two ends and you have a belt loop, attach three edges and you have a pocket. Incorporate the skill of appliqué into the design of the dress, don't just think of it as an extra.

If you use motifs, don't choose a design where the outline is too wiggly. Keep it simple. What motifs to use? You can use anything to continue your theme, but if you are planning to use white on white, some traditional motifs might be: doves, snowflakes, horseshoes, balloons, hearts, bows or stars.

If you wish to be more adventurous, why not appliqué one of the most famous fictional weddings of all time: the owl and the pussy cat? The motifs to use are simple; the owl, the cat, the pea green boat, a ring, a pig (with a ring through the end of his nose), and a moon. Why not have a different motif on each bridesmaid's dress and an entire scene (such as dancing by the light of the moon) on the ring cushion? What could be more unique?

The technique of appliqué will allow you to use minimal amounts of material in strategic places. If you have only a tiny piece of old-fashioned lace, perhaps from your christening gown, or from your grandmother's wedding dress, you can appliqué it to the bodice of your dress and know your gown combines sentiment and originality.

Appliqué will add to the weight of a garment and give it more body. Consider how your design could benefit from two or three layers, maybe at the hem or across the bodice. Appliqué doesn't have to be one layer on another. You can build up several layers of fabric. It's at this point, applying layers of material to a surface, where appliqué can become quilting.

You don't have to sew around all the edges of your motif, as the illustrations show. Picking where you wish to sew and *what you wish to leave free will give you a frill, hoops to thread a sash through or even pockets.*

Appliqué. You can use a simple running stitch to attach your motif to the backing cloth (horseshoe) or a more decorative embroidery stitch such as cross stitch (bow) to make it more interesting.

Alternatively, apply a layer of lace or braid over the edges of your motif (heart) and perhaps hide untidy stitches.

Quilting

Quilting is ancient, attractive and sumptuous. It is also quite simple. Throughout the ages the techniques have remained largely the same: putting two layers of material together, with perhaps a thin layer of wadding or wool between them, then holding them firmly together with a pattern of simple running stitches or machine stitching. I have seen it referred to as a 'textile sandwich', and that is just what it is.

Before the advent of central heating, ladies who wished to wear gowns of silk or satin could do so in comfort when they quilted them. They could mince along in the finest of silks in the dead of winter because their gown and petticoats were several layers thick and padded with wool. Modern brides can reap the same advantages. Winter brides should think hard about stylish little jackets or embroidered and padded boleros. Little boys and girls will look miserable in the photographs if they get cold. Keep them warm with padded jackets or body-warmers.

Avoid running the risk of thinking of quilting only in terms of anoraks or soft furnishings! It doesn't have to be like that. Quilting doesn't just provide thickness, it gives us texture and the interplay of light and shadow. Any dress or suit that has shoulder pads or epaulettes can be lightly quilted. Cuffs, yokes and belts can all be textured using this interesting craft. Quilting may seem unusual to include in a wedding gown, but on the right garment it can look magnificent.

It can also be useful. Ladies with flat chests may like to soften and round the front panel of their dress and emboss it with embroidery and beads. Exchange your dissatisfaction with your shape into pride at a queen-like gown.

And what about the groom? Why not make him a grey silk waistcoat using the thinnest of wadding (if any), and machine embroider random patterns or 'squiggles' to make it look richly

A number of ways to use quilting.

textured. Pageboys, too, could be dressed like this. Once again, quilting adds weight and body to a garment; consider whether this will be useful for your style of garment. Bow ties, sashes, purses, bags, satin slippers and caps are all items that can be quilted and lifted out of the ordinary.

There are different types of quilting and one that is particularly simple is Italian quilting. Here the design is made by sewing two layers of fabric together with parallel rows of stitches to outline your chosen pattern. The padding is put in later by running a cord or length of thick wool between the two rows of stitches. If you use fine fabrics like muslin or thin cotton and insert coloured wools, you will find you get a softly padded, pastel-shadowed piece of quilting.

Trapinto quilting is even simpler as only the design is stuffed. You use running stitch or back stitch to outline, for example, a dove on your two layers of cloth. All you do then is cut a slit in the backing layer and poke in some stuffing. Voilà! A stuffed motif.

Don't fall into the trap of overstuffing. The dandies of the sixteenth century so padded their clothes to give themselves the appearance of a broad chest or well-muscled thighs that the padding alone weighed pounds! Many a leader of male fashion was made to faint through overheating.

If you use a motif for quilting, perhaps a heart, remember that it doesn't have to be padded everywhere you use it. Use the same motif as decorative embroidery. You will see in the photograph below that the bridesmaids each have heart motifs applied to their dresses at thigh and calf but only some of them are quilted. This adds variety while maintaining the style.

Here all the bridesmaids have heart motifs applied and embroidered at thigh and calf. Note that the young lady in the foreground has a quilted heart on her dress. I particularly like the fact that the bridesmaids also wear little veils.

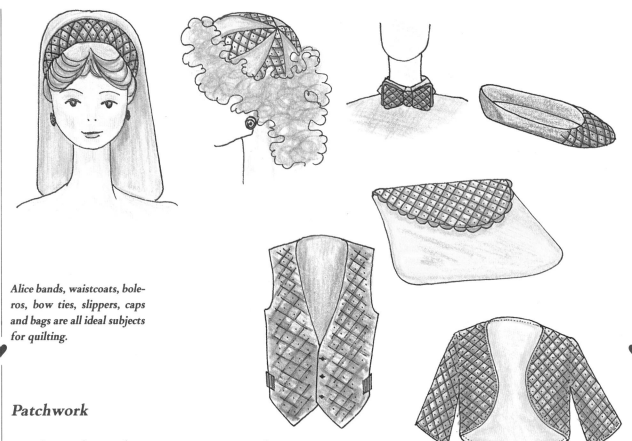

Alice bands, waistcoats, bole- ros, bow ties, slippers, caps and bags are all ideal subjects for quilting.

Patchwork

For those of you who turn up your toes in horror at the thought of a patchwork bridal gown, I beg you to consider one or two thoughts. Patchwork is not only for quilts, it can be for anything. For centuries women have been proving their ingenuity and artistry by joining together scraps of fabric to make items which were both decorative and useful.

The most important feature of patchwork is that it uses small pieces of fabric (it was once a byword for thrift) and this is the aspect of it that we can usefully exploit. You can use tiny amounts of expensive fabrics by mixing them with cheaper materials. Another good feature of patchwork, and why I think it is suitable for a modern bride, is its ability to create or utilise items of sentiment.

Patchwork 'sewing bees' were usually a community or social celebration: the entire community gathered together to help a bride complete her bottom drawer or to create an item that commemorated a marriage or birth. Some clever entrepreneurs printed commemorative squares for inclusion into quilts for all major events from royal marriages to victorious battles. Whether or not your man put up a fight, you too can use items or scraps of fabric that are special to you.

The first thing patchwork beginners ever make is a cushion. So let's make the ring cushion from patches. If you have made your own dress, use scraps from that or use remnants of your mother's or grandmother's gown to include in the cushion. Include bits from the bridesmaids' dresses to add touches of colour.

Alternatively you can do the obvious and opt for making a quilt; but do it American style. Get all your female (and even male) relatives to embroider or decorate squares of a quilt. Then, before the wedding, have a sewing bee and join the whole thing up. Cement family ties, let people get to know each other before the big day, have fun and don't worry that the stitches are a little tipsy! Display the quilt with pride at the reception.

If you like cats or have a 'cat' theme for your wedding then you must use patchwork somewhere! Many American traditional quilting patterns were given 'cat' names such as 'puss in boots' or 'puss in the corner'. It's a lovely and subtle way to introduce a cat theme.

Patchwork techniques can make use of the tiniest scraps of exotic fabrics in a host of different ways.

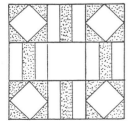 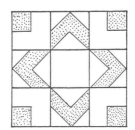

Traditional 'cat' patchwork patterns: puss in the corner (far left); puss in boots (centre); kitty corner (left).

Smocking

Smocking has become an English folk art but arose out of quite practical considerations when making working clothes. Smocking is a skill that combines the gathering of pleats and subsequent decoration with embroidery. The appearance of the fabric's surface and the whole shape of a garment can be changed by using smocking. Originally it was used to control the fullness of a garment made for farm workers. It was almost incidental that the technique added other facets such as waterproofing and beauty!

Any garment that has fullness pulled into gathers can be smocked. Before smocking, the area to be worked is marked out with dots and one can buy iron-on transfers of dots of various spacings or gauges for this.

In original smocks the embroidery work was often personalised. The plain 'boxes' on either side of the smocked area were filled with motifs that reflected the wearer's profession or were peculiar to their family or village. There are books that go into the subject in depth and give many traditional patterns, some especially for weddings. Why not complete the olde English feel of your wedding by putting your pageboys or bridesmaids in traditional smocks? There are even one or two companies that make them if you like the style but don't fancy the work. Round the day off by hiring Morris dancers to perform on the front lawn. Since Morris dancing contains a host of fertility rituals, what could be better for a wedding?

Smocking isn't just restricted to yokels' smocks; it can be used in many places. Moreover, smocking isn't just the gathering of material; its additional beauty comes from the intricacy of the embroidery pattern put on it. Don't forget that you can be really stylish and unique here – colours, different threads and beads can all be included to make one small area of smocking into a work of art.

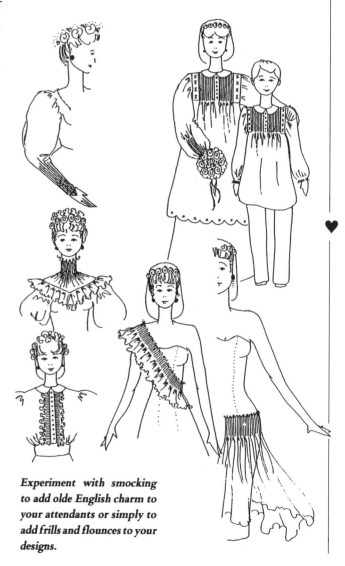

Experiment with smocking to add olde English charm to your attendants or simply to add frills and flounces to your designs.

Since smocking 'gathers up' spare cloth, it is useful for altering the fit of something. Emphasise a tiny waist by pulling in loose fabric on a straight dress or make jumble sale gloves fit better by smocking their backs. Don't just gather up your veil and attach it to a comb: pleat it and smock it with silver embroidery and beads to create a headdress and veil in one.

Make a simple fan or rosette by drawing one edge of a piece of cloth together. Smock it, bead it, add tassels and suddenly you can carry a fan instead of flowers. Make a rosette or half-rosette and use it as a detail on your dress. If you attach it to a comb you have a hair ornament, maybe even a French maid's saucy cap?

Bows can be made by gathering the middle of a rectangular piece of cloth. Why leave it there? Smock it instead to make very stylish little bows to use on your dress, in the bridesmaids' hair or as stunning bow ties for the pageboys.

Some of my favourite designs for dresses, and methods of re-fashioning an old dress include the use of smocking. The illustrations show some designs that have smocking as decoration or have pieces of smocked material added to give them a new style.

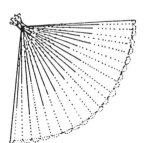

Using smocking to gather and shape fabric as well as to decorate.

You can use smocking as a main feature of a garment or simply to gather, shape and decorate.

Crochet

You may think that crochet dresses should be left in the 1970s when they really came into vogue. Nevertheless, crochet is a skill that many of us possess and could, indeed should, be used creatively. Actually, it has to be said that someone with the right figure – thin – can look stunning in a simple clinging gown that emulates the 1930s Hollywood starlet look.

Crochet is sometimes known as nuns' lace. This is because the common lacy form of crochet was developed in Italy in the sixteenth century when nuns created it to use as trimmings for church vestments. It is this lacy aspect of crochet that we can best exploit for weddings.

Be creative. Don't simply pop down to the local knitting shop and buy a 1990s pattern. Go to your aunt's or grandmother's house and plunder their knitting baskets. Do they have any patterns for crocheted lace that date from the war years or earlier? Send dad up in the loft to look through the old magazines gathering dust up there. Tour junk shops and book sellers; they often have copies of old magazines with very intricate patterns in them. The work of the early patterns was so much finer then as wool and yarn were much thinner.

Nowadays we have a whole panoply of man-made fibres, threads and yarns to use. We can use thin hooks and fine thread to make cobweb-fine lace, or fat hooks and thick yarn for making dense fabrics for hats, bags and slippers. But you aren't restricted to using cotton, wool or yarn. Try ribbons, raffia or even green garden twine! (The latter would be excellent for making ropes or doilies to decorate with flowers for the church.)

Crochet can produce the finest lace, Consider where you might use it to best advantage.

This bride's hands are protected by dainty crocheted gloves which complement her knitted dress.

For the amateur I would not recommend making a whole gown, but do suggest that crochet is a quick and satisfying method of producing hand-made, unusual lace. A simple crochet edging can be used most effectively in a number of ways on a dress, and remember that a strip of crocheted lace can be made a little more special and original by sewing little pearls, tiny beads or delicate droplets on it.

A simple white lace collar, for example, when used on a red velvet dress with a red satin sash, is quite stunning. Wear little white gloves (crocheted, of course) and you will be a winter bride who will chase away the chill of the weather. Reproduce the look in your bridesmaids' costumes and don't be afraid to use jewel-bright or daringly-dark fabrics for the dresses to show off your hand-made lace.

The use of crochet is not confined to the production of clothes. You can make large doilies and use them as lacy backings for your bouquet and the bridesmaids' posies. Or you can crochet little caps for the bridesmaids and a shawl for yourself. Make three-dimensional roses and put them everywhere.

See if you can find a really easy crochet motif to use and then make dozens at leisure. You can make them while you're watching TV, when you're commuting, or during your lunch hour. Then, at your wedding, you'll have hand-made drinks coasters for each of your guests; a much nicer keepsake than a book of matches. Join several motifs together and drape the cake table in hand-made lace. You will find many motifs that may suit your theme from snowflakes to stars, from rainbows to roses.

Knitting

Knitting, of course, is very much like crochet and modern brides may balk at the thought of making a knitted wedding dress – indeed, so would I! Mind you, it is possible with machine knitting and devotees of the art are quite capable of using their skills in producing lovely wedding wear. The knitted dress featured in the photograph on page 54 was designed by a knitting club and made up by one of their members for a fashion show.

But we must not overlook hand knitting. It is an exciting skill and with so many wonderful yarns and fibres at our fingertips, there is no reason not to use this skill in producing the most fantastic and luxurious garments or possessions.

Of all the skills I have mentioned here, knitting is probably the most ancient. Knitted items have been found that date from 500 AD, though the experts declare that knitting was a skill used at least a thousand years before Christ was born. In the middle ages there were guilds of knitters (almost all of them male) who were seen as master craftsmen every bit as skilled as goldsmiths or artists.

Although knitting is old, it is not old-fashioned; it can be witty and stylish. Libraries and shops abound with books on the subject. Look through Kaffe Fassett, Wildlife Knitting or other designer-knit books for inspiration. Why not give your guests a laugh and knit a copy of your wedding cake and stand it beside the real thing? Each tier can later be used as a cushion for your bed or sofa. Then again, you can knit dolls for your Victorian-style bridesmaids to carry, or perhaps even a whole woolly bouquet.

In case you are wondering how knitting can fit in with my philosophy of being unique, can I remind you that some items of knitwear are so distinctive they are universally recognised? Witness the Guernsey pullover. Some families or villages had their own distinctive stitch patterns to make them even more unique. Actually, Guernsey jumpers started out being called 'bridal shirts' because all the girls made one for their betrothed for the wedding day.

If you think that knitting is only suited to the thick and bulky Guernsey or Aran sweaters, you may be surprised to learn that some examples of hand knitting boast thirty-six stitches to the inch!

Whether you use your knitting skills to make a garment or a lacy trim you can't help but stamp your personality and artistry on the day.

— 52 —

The finest work we are likely to knit has perhaps only ten stitches to the inch.

Now, having exploded some of the myths about knitting, let's look at how you can use it.

Knitted garments are simply wonderful to wear. What winter bride would not look fetching (and warm) in a little knitted jacket, prettied with shoulder bows copied from Sarah Ferguson's dress? Alternatively, a white mohair bolero can be made extra special by sewing little pearls on to it.

Dress your attendants in matching pastel-coloured boleros to keep out the chill of a spring morning.

Consider wearing a starkly plain white gown and wear a large shawl of the finest gossamer thread. Add a few sequins or beads to this cobweb-fine garment and raise it out of the ordinary to become something really stylish. Highlight the workmanship of such a delicate garment by wearing it over a dark gown – midnight blue or indigo satin.

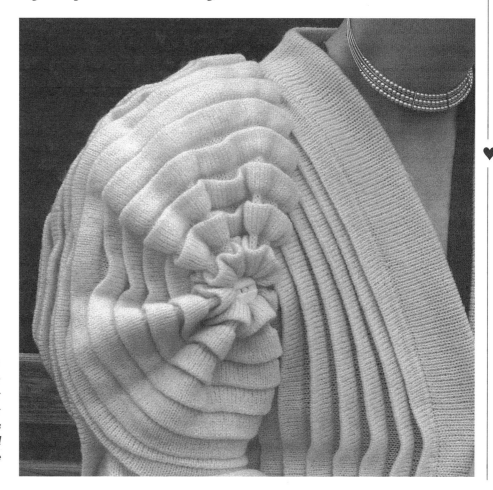

Detail of the knitted jacket on page 54. (Jacket is No. 7 of the Zandra Rhodes Collection by Brother. It was knitted by Janet Purvis of Dropinstitches in three-ply Forsell pure wool on a Brother standard gauge machine.)

Once again, old patterns are a particular joy. It will be worth scouring the bookshops if you find an original 1940s pattern which allows you to adopt a post-war style by wearing a beautifully tailored knitted jacket and matching beret.

Are you limited to a budget wedding? Dress your pageboys in their school uniform shirts and trousers, but top them off with a smart knitted waistcoat and toning bow tie. Use a plain rib stitch at the back for a good fit but use interesting patterns or exotic yarns for the front. Black, ruby or jade 'mohair' yarn would look special, or perhaps you could use one of the many bobbly or tufted yarns available. Visit the shops and see if something inspires you.

Left: An example of how exquisite knitting can be: a wedding dress in two-ply yarn. (The dress was knitted by Joyce Canon for a Dropin-stitches fashion show on a Knit Master 360 with an automatic lace carriage.)

Above: This stunning jacket is machine knitted and perfect for the register office bride who has to face the chill of autumn.

Chapter 3

Buttons, Bows and Furbelows

*'For talk six times with the same single lady, and you may get
the wedding dresses ready.'*
BYRON

It is debatable whether choosing the wedding dress is the most important part of planning a wedding, but in my opinion it is certainly the most fun. There is magic in finding the gown that will turn Jane Doe into Princess Jane for the day, and there is satisfaction in finding the dress that will give her the confidence to stroll up the aisle to gasps of admiration, and make her groom fall in love with her all over again.

The bride's outfit is an important item of the wedding because it is the one item (apart from the groom) that has the power to make a nervous young bride feel good about herself. Whatever you wear is right as long as it makes you feel good. This is so important I can't stress it enough. On the big day you and your groom will be the centre of attention and you must feel comfortable and at ease in order to enjoy the day. If your chosen outfit makes you feel like one of the ugly sisters, or if you feel a little under-dressed or over-dressed, then change it.

Choosing a Style

There are many ways that you can stamp your own personal style on your wedding, and the dress, of course, is an obvious place to start.

If you have already chosen a theme to link the various aspects of your wedding, you will want to include it in your dress. Of course, it may be that you want the style of the dress to set the theme. Your choice of a 1920s dress, or perhaps a dress with a Spanish influence, will very likely have repercussions on your choice of bridesmaids' dresses and flowers.

But choosing a style isn't necessarily that easy. Just about any national costume, any TV programme or movie can be exploited as inspiration for a style of wedding dress. There are many styles that you can adopt, so many that you may be bewildered by the scale of choice. Start simply by thumbing through magazines and then visiting bridal shops and looking at their collections. Most shops carry a stock that ranges from the simplest of styles right through to the stunning and extravagant. You may well find that it is at this point, when you spot the dress of your dreams, that the form and style of your wedding comes sharply into focus.

As a beginning, remember that we have several thousand years of history behind us from which to choose a style. Within that period of time there must be one image that you would wish to capture and reproduce. As an exercise, I have sketched eighteen different historical styles and have discussed how you can use or adapt them. Have a look and see if they spark any ideas for you.

You may think it is unlikely that you will be able to buy similar history-inspired styles off-the-peg, but you will. There are endless designers who specialise in particular styles of gown and whether you are looking for 1920s, art nouveau, medieval or Victorian styles you are bound to find someone who sells them.

Don't forget that chain stores and the well known bridal wear companies offer dresses that reflect different fashion styles. Just about every wedding collection incorporates a dress that harks back to the Edwardian era or the roundheads and cavaliers. You may not have to go to an independent designer to get what you want and you may not have to break the bank either.

Diana, Aphrodite and Athene

These are Greek or Roman in inspiration and would be stunning on a bride or bridesmaids for sheer novelty. Although rather unusual they could, in the right materials, be incredibly cheap. If you have dozens of potential bridesmaids, this could be a way of decking them out on a budget.

A richer, more sophisticated look could be achieved for a bride by using an expensive fabric: silk, sari material or lace. To protect one's modesty and to make it easier to wear, the addition of a simple lining would give the dress some structure

Diana, Aphrodite and Athene.

and allow a fine fabric to float and swish. Don't forget that softly draped styles readily lend themselves to modern fabrics such as cotton jersey or man-made jersey fabrics. An autumn or winter wedding could be made warmer by the use of the latter with long sleeves, soft drapes across the breasts and a cape of pleats down the back.

Marian, Eleanor and Guinevere.

wore togas trimmed with a purple band to identify their rank.) Plait three different coloured ribbons together or, for an innocent vestal virgin air, wind flowers into the braid. This could look particularly charming on your bridesmaids.

Headdresses could be simple wreaths of white flowers, perhaps just gypsophila. I don't wish to suggest laurel leaves, but a simple circlet of greenery would look good too.

Marian, Eleanor and Guinevere

These Maid Marian or Norman conquest ideas are quite simple to make and would lend a most unique flavour to your wedding. You might like to consider them if you are marrying in a Norman church. Perhaps these styles are ideal for the modern lady who dislikes all the frills and furbelows that are often associated with wedding gowns.

For these styles, cotton jersey just begs to be used, as do soft pastel colours. Don't forget that some man-made jerseys have self patterns and bright sheens to them, which could enhance the simple lines of these dresses and give them a positively regal air. Velour or velvet would work well in these styles for a winter wedding.

The shoulder rolls and headdresses are simply tubes of cloth stuffed and bound with braid, contrasting cloth or strings of pearls. The skirts can be left slim and elegant, hiding the fact that it is easier to make them that way. Or, if your dressmaking skills and sewing machine are up to it, you can make the skirt as full as you wish by using a pattern with many panels.

To complete the picture, use antique brooches or reproduction jewellery as clasps. There are many shops and catalogues that sell copies of period jewellery.

Think about the trimming. A colourful or rich braid would add life to a plain white gown, although purple would evoke memories of the Roman Senate! (Members of the Roman Senate

Elizabeth.

The 'Eleanor' design is plainness itself and, whilst I hate to admit it, not suitable for those of us who are less than lean. However, disguise its inherent plainness by wearing a heavily jewelled girdle. Make this in a contrasting fabric – satin or taffeta – and cover it with pearls, lace and beading.

'Guinevere' may be a little more difficult to achieve but lends itself to the use of contrasting and different fabrics. It would also be a good way of disguising broad hips or advancing pregnancy. My illustration has braided trimming, but imagine it made from plain white cotton jersey from top to toe – but with big white satin roses positioned close together around the neckline – sumptuous.

Any Saxon or Norman lady of the manor worth her salt would have carried a hawk on her arm, but this is perhaps something you cannot emulate. Instead, consider carrying richly decorated gauntlets, a posy of herbs or a Bible.

Elizabeth

This Tudor design could be such a lot of fun. The period immediately suggests the use of rich and regal fabrics – which means that straight away you can rummage through off-cut bins for remnants of embroidered satins, brocades, laces, velvets and satins.

Other aspects to think about are ruffs and frills. Personally, I wouldn't bother trying to produce perfect starched ruffs (although there are some very good stage costume books that will tell you how). Instead you could use several layers of the many pre-gathered lace trimmings that are available.

Nell.

Slash the sleeves. Be daring and slash through sleeves to reveal another fabric and another colour beneath. What a perfect place to introduce your colour theme. Heavy embroidery on the front panel is almost obligatory, so find a very intricate pattern and give it your best efforts as you embroider and bead it. Perhaps you have a small piece of very rich fabric that you want to include – a remnant of your christening robe, a piece of your mother's gown – use it here.

Why not hang pomanders, fans, keys or good luck charms on ribbons at your waist and carry embroidered gloves or gauntlets? Headdresses could range from anything from crowns or wreaths to an Anne Boleyn snood.

Nell

It's a fair jump from Elizabeth to Nell Gwynn, but both dresses could share the same dress patterns.

Materials to use here would be satins and silks. You could use the finest silks over a crinoline petticoat and waft up the aisle. Alternatively, with a budget on your mind, you could use a cheap lining for the underskirt with perhaps a layer of equally cheap dress-net over that. Use skimpy measures of a more precious fabric like satin or sari fabric as an overskirt, draw it back in soft folds and tie it with huge satin bows. Introduce your colour theme in the underskirt and highlight it in your ribbon trim. Overload the bodice with cotton-type lace, several layers deep. Remember Nell Gwynn and expose a healthy cleavage.

A picture hat crowned with flowers, perhaps tied with chiffon under the chin, would look very well, as would a traditional veil and tiara. But what is your hair like? Don't overlook your own best features: as long as you don't end up looking like a cocker spaniel, consider ringlets and ribbons in your hair. Modern perms can emulate this look very well.

To carry? How about a formal bouquet or a tiny trug or basket of roses (not oranges as Nell is usually pictured with!). A fan, gloves or a Bible would also fit the part.

Purity

Someone who looks or feels silly in frills, or is marrying in a simple church should consider this puritan style. If simplicity is your natural preference, don't get caught up in the over-kill of fashion – stay simple.

Purity.

Although evocative of Cromwell and the roundheads, this style doesn't have to be made in grey flannel. It could be made in any number of exotic fabrics, but its simple lines and easy-sew

style can carry a plain white satin. My preference would be for a dove grey taffeta with white lace collar, cuffs and trimmings with pearl details. Consider carrying a Bible, prayer book or a simple sheaf of flowers.

Scarlett and Belle

These are my Scarlett O'Hara styles – history gone Hollywood. Imagine how 'King and I-like' you will feel sweeping around the floor with your new husband when you take the first dance in such a crinolined creation. Scarlett is the simplest and it is only the choice of material and trim that make it exotic. I have illustrated contrasting, draped ribbons with a ribbon sash, but these could equally be frills or lace trimming. A Scarlett O'Hara picture hat could work but the dress style does lend itself to a traditional tiara and veil.

Belle and Scarlett.

'Belle' could be made in the obvious wedding fabrics but you could also consider using very fine cotton with a tiny print. Choose a saucy little hat with a veil and steal the show.

For both these dresses, gloves are a must. But you don't have to wear them, just carry them. Draw-string bags or the tiniest of parasols could look very fetching.

Josephine

Wellington or Bonaparte would have loved a bride in this dress. Historically these dresses were made in soft muslin, often dampened to cling to

Josephine.

the body and reveal a lack of underclothes! There are many fabrics you can buy today to emulate the style, if not the morals, of Regency England. The style is also ideal for bridesmaids of any age.

If the weather promises to be cool, wear it with a spencer, a little velvet jacket which comes just under the bust. Adorn the front with frogging and

repeat the trim on the cavalry uniform of your pageboys.

Consider whether you want to leave the neckline bare to show off the antique pendant borrowed from your grandmother. However, if you are coy about showing too much cleavage it is also correct to wear the style with lace inserts that come all the way up to your chin. Carry a dolly-bag, fan or parasol.

Sarah

Sarah Bernhardt was a well known figure of the theatre. This dress is simple to make and, in fact, uses much the same pattern as the 'Nell Gwynne' and 'Scarlett' dresses. The style is one that lends itself to a long train, which can either be shaped as part of the skirt or made as a detachable apron train. The dress can be made wholly from one quality fabric or with a sheer fabric over a cheaper lining. Emphasise the daringly bare shoulders

Sarah.

with a plain ribbon choker at your throat. Decide upon a cheeky bow on your backside and decorate the bow with lace, beads and ribbons.

Carry a feathery fan, a huge bouquet or just a pair of gloves.

Mary

Queen Mary was tall and slim. Make yourself look taller by adopting these elegant lines rather than choosing the teapot shape of a crinoline as in

Mary.

'Scarlett' or 'Belle'. You should be able to find endless dress patterns for this style so there is no chance of claiming it is too difficult.

This will look absolutely splendid in cream or ivory lace. You can tackle it in two ways: either make the dress with a cheap lining covered with a lightweight lace, or make it in a heavier, more expensive lace and wear it over a simple straight-

Above: A short dress for a church ceremony is not commonly seen, but it is perfect for this bride and she has taken the opportunity to show off her very pretty shoes. Don't couples always look radiant coming down the aisle?

Above: A bridal gown in true romantic fashion. A full train with lace inserts and a short veil with blusher complete the image of the perfect bride.

This dress combines satin and lace to give an elegant look for the bride who likes the traditional romantic style of gown but wants to avoid too many frills and ribbons.

cut shift. Either way will look authentic. Add umpteen pearl buttons-and-loops down the back, or hide a zip with fake pearl buttons.

Pile your hair high, wear a tiara and carry an enormous fan or bouquet.

Millie and Vera

'Millie' and 'Vera', a flapper and a GI-Bride, are relatively modern styles.

The years of the 1920s and 30s had a mood all of their own: capture it with cloche hats, strings of pearls, straight dresses and fringes. Search flea markets, boot sales and antique shops for the real thing, but if you can't find an original, simply make up a straight dress and decorate it into style.

Vera and Millie

The style of a flapper dress is simplicity itself to make and is ideal for those trying to disguise the lack of a waist or bust or advancing pregnancy. Remember that no amount of beads, fringes or sequins can be over the top on a flapper dress. If this is the sort of dress you want, don't buy it, this is one you must make! No other bride in the world will ever be the same as you.

The flapper can be soft and unstructured or bright and glitzy, take your choice. Headdresses can be stylish cloche hats or soft veils draped over the blushing bride with a circlet of flowers.

If you have decided on a short dress, this is an ideal style to adopt. Remember, with short dresses your shoes can be stunning. Invest in shoes of the period if you can. If not, buy plain satin court shoes (dyed to match if necessary) and add bows and beads.

Marry an Al Capone groom and have pageboys in knickerbockers, braces and flat caps. Ride in a period car. Consider putting the ushers in dark suits and homburg hats and give them violin cases to add a touch of humour to the photos!

World War Two brides also had a look all their own. Ask your mum or aunts or gran what they wore. They will probably tell you that it was parachute silk. My mother-in-law's trousseau was largely made of parachute silk and she still has a piece!

I'm lucky enough to have a wedding dress pattern that dates from just after the war – 1949; it's terrific. Remember that war-time evening dresses were silky and smooth and shapely – very feminine, very sexy. If the styles of the post-war wedding dresses don't take your fancy, why not copy a war-time evening dress?

Carry flowers with masses of trailing greenery and make sure you dance to Glen Miller tunes.

Diana and Fergie

These are, of course, the more recent Royals and though their weddings may have been forgotten among more recent negative publicity, they still give us valuable lessons in style which we can use to our advantage.

Both the royal brides were stunning, each in their different way. As a student of bridal fashions I saw how Diana's dress changed the face of weddings. Frills and flounces were immediately the order of the day for every bride and bridal boutique. She did away with the sameness of weddings and gave us a fairy tale style.

Fergie and Diana.

Fergie was totally different and still stunning. She gets my vote for being a unique bride for her originality in incorporating their initials, S and A, in the embroidery on the dress. Some cried it was corny, but I loved it. She was being different, ensuring it was personal to her and not worrying what the rest of the world thought. It was, after all, her wedding.

Both royal brides had creamy white flowers and Sarah wore a heavy fresh-flower headdress –it worked well for them, but I would opt for a more varied colour scheme. You don't want to be accused of copying; after all, we are striving for originality here.

Using a Family Dress

Many brides choose to use a dress that has been worn before. Whilst in some areas of the country people feel that traditionally the gown should be the 'something new' for a bride, it is also appealing to wear something that was worn at the start of another happy marriage. Such a dress doesn't have to be a pre-Victorian lace heirloom, it can simply be your mother's or grandmother's dress. I know one bride who was the fourth bride to wear a dress dating from the 1940s. The dress belonged to her aunt and was made from Nottingham lace. Moreover, she is not likely to be the last to wear it as another member of the family has asked her to put it by safely so that she can wear it later. This particular bride also had the original veil and headdress, but chose to buy her own to stamp her individuality on the ensemble.

There is no doubt that there are fashions to

wedding dresses and some gowns will look more dated than others. You may find that you'll have to up-date a borrowed dress to make it feel and look special instead of simply second-hand.

When you borrow a dress, or refurbish a junk-shop find, look carefully at it and see how you can improve upon it. A change of lace or braid may give a whole new lease of life to a dress. So too will washing it with fabric brighteners and changing buttons and zips. If the fabric is dull and not improved by washing, then consider dyeing it a subtle colour to hide the signs of age.

Buying or making new undergarments such as petticoats will give a freshness to old dresses and relining an old dress will give it instant vitality.

It's unlikely that a borrowed dress will fit you perfectly, so you will have to make some alterations to it. Do take care how you do this and do nothing too drastic as other people may want it after you.

Buying a Dress

There is no doubt that shopping for a wedding dress can be a bit of a trial. It can be hot and exhausting and quite dispiriting. But do not be intimidated by the shops. Some, I know, have the air of funeral parlours and are quite off-putting, and some have sales staff who try and convince a bride that she looks so much nicer in the styles that cost the most. Take courage and remember: they are there to sell dresses and you are a potential buyer. You have a right to buy exactly what you want and can keep looking until you find it.

Fortunately, most shops are more than happy for you to climb in and out of as many dresses as you can bear (though some may not let you try on very expensive dresses unless you are fairly interested in buying). You may find your size 14 body crammed into a communal size 10 used for fittings — but you'll get an idea of how you look. You'll also find that most assistants will be helpful and full of suggestions for dress styles or accessories you would not otherwise have considered.

It is traditional for the bride to go dress-buying with her mother, and possibly her mother-in-law. Take care. I would advise any young bride to go out with a friend first. Go with the girls from work or, if you have a friend with outrageous tastes, take her! Let yourself be persuaded into trying on dresses that you'd never dream would suit you.

I went wedding-dress shopping with certain ideas in mind but, with each passing dress, that image changed. I took my English pear shape along to several bridal shops in the company of my sister-in-law, who forced me into all sorts of unsuitable dresses to oblige her sense of humour. She coerced me into a very slim-fitting Edwardian dress complete with bustle and swathe of silk across the hips. In spite of my lack of height, and in spite of the width of my hips, it looked magnificent. I felt like something out of *My Fair Lady*. I was just about to snap it up when she made me try on another. It is as well that she did, for we found the design that was 'me' and I knew I could stop looking.

Don't be forced by the salesgirl, your friends or your mother into anything which doesn't feel right. You'll have enough to occupy your nerves

When you're looking for your dream dress, you'll find that the stores offer gowns at both ends of the style spectrum. Above is an intricate, elegant gown that contrasts nicely with the simpler more traditional gown on the left.

on the day without feeling worried about how you look.

When you find the right dress, you'll know it. It will feel like the you of your dreams. It will make you feel like a million dollars, yet you wouldn't feel out of place doing the washing-up in it! I make wedding dresses. I get a kick out of making an ordinary young woman carry herself like a queen because her gown makes her feel like something from a fairy tale. But I like it even more when that same young woman hitches her skirt up to her knees, flings the train over her arm and engages in an impromptu game of tag with the pageboys.

Feel at home in your dress and comfortable with the style you adopt. Don't try to emulate a big society wedding if you're happiest being a small-town girl. If you like wearing modern casual clothes and dread the thought of having to dress up in a posh white frock – don't. Go to the chain stores and see what's around. Why not team up some wide-legged pants with an unstructured jacket in natural or muted shades? Tour the hat shops or junk shops until you find a hat, perhaps a soft wide-brimmed hat, that lifts these street clothes out of the ordinary.

Be guided by others but let the final choice be your own. When you find the dress or outfit you want, buy it and enjoy it.

Having said all that and having suggested you find a style that is 'you', it may be that you cannot afford the dress you want, or that the shops simply do not sell it. If this is the case, consider hiring it or making it.

If you are hiring a dress, the principles are the same as if you are buying. Look round, try on and choose carefully. Allow plenty of time as you will need to book the dress well in advance to avoid disappointment. Have your booking confirmation in writing and make sure you pay the required deposits and the outstanding balance on time.

Making a Dress

It is said that it is unlucky to make your own wedding dress. All I can say to this is that I know several brides who made their own dresses and they seem to be thriving. Ruby Moore, for instance, made her wedding dress in 1935 and she is still happy, healthy and with the man she married. That can't be bad luck!

To offset any possibility of bad luck, you could choose to wear a lucky blue dress or make sure something blue is included in it. I ensure that all my brides' dresses have a blue bow or blue rose sewn into the hem.

Another reason people shy away from making a wedding dress is because it is special and something out of the ordinary. I realise that many of you believe it will be impossible for you, and are probably thinking things like: 'I can't sew, I haven't done anything like that since school....'. But do think about it. It needn't be difficult and it will make your wedding dress so very special and your wedding day unique.

There is a lot of fun to be had in making a dress. Picking the pattern, finding the material and choosing the trimmings are just the early stages. Cutting out can be a bit of a chore, just as pinning and tacking it into its first stages can be. But when you see the dress begin to take shape under your hands you won't regret it. You'll be pleased as punch and twice as proud!

Gather the materials, the sewing machine, the bride and the dressmaker together and find a nice quiet spot. Of course, if the bride and dressmaker are the same person, then you must find yourself a helper; you can't do it by yourself, you have to share the work. Add some favourite music, put a fresh-cream treat in the fridge for later, open a bottle of sherry and see if you don't have fun!

Approach the making of your dress as though it will be fun, and it will be. From the word go, your dress will be cut, stitched and fitted with laughter and there will be pleasure in almost every stitch. When you finally wear it, any worries you may have had about a home-made dress, will have long turned to dust.

But if you feel you really are unable to sew it yourself, ask friends and relatives if they will do the honours. Although thousands of mothers have had sleepless nights because they volunteered to make the dress, and then had fits of worries about whether it would be good enough, those same women almost burst with pride when they see their daughter in the dress at the altar.

Of course, the local papers carry details of people like myself who are happy to make the gown of your dreams for you. I enjoy making wedding dresses more than any other garment. When asked if it is difficult, I have to be honest and reply that it is not as hard as people imagine. It is quite simple to run up a little white number, drape lace across it in luxurious folds, and stand back and watch everyone swoon in amazement.

Use pattern books to their best advantage. The pattern companies are bang up to date with fashion and style, but can also be relied upon to offer the traditional. Here, just one pattern gives you five basic designs to mull over. Choose the most elaborate for the bride and adapt simpler versions for the bridesmaids.

PATTERN/PATRON **1511**

Home-made dresses don't have to be plain and simple, as these lusciously elegant designs show. Be stunningly different in your own creation that still boasts a designer's name.

Indeed, I had one young bride come for a fitting, and she went into raptures when she saw the dress on the dummy, claiming that it was everything she'd ever dreamed of. Her jaw dropped a moment later as I took out the pins that were holding it together, and she saw that her wonderful dress was still a collection of pattern pieces that hadn't even been sewn together! Beauty is certainly in the eye of the beholder.

Some wedding dresses, like stage costumes, are simple to make because there are many ways of disguising any errors under all the frills and flounces. Making a straight, fitted skirt is much harder by comparison and requires much more skill.

Whilst I am sure that dressmakers of repute will shudder at some of the things I advocate here, this section is not for them but for the average home dressmaker. Professionals know exactly what they are doing and need no advice from me. They will follow the correct dressmaking procedures. I hope that I can convince the amateur seamstress, however, that dressmaking is a flexible art and that it is possible to build a dress to startle the world without being an expert. Get rid of some preconceived notions, un-learn some of the things you may have been taught and have a go! Creating a dream dress is probably well within your capabilities, so do be tempted to try.

Once you have decided on the style of your dress, don't despair if the local dressmaking shop doesn't have a pattern for it. A competent dressmaker, if you are using one, should be able to manage without an exact pattern and cut her own. If you are making the dress yourself, don't give up if you can't find the precise pattern. You can mix and match bits of others to make it; remember a gown is only a collection of sleeves, a bodice and a skirt. You may have to buy a maximum of three patterns to get bits that are suitable. You may even have patterns at home that will do. You don't have to do the obvious. You can have a dress that is exactly what you want.

A tailor or dressmaker will tell you that you shouldn't mix and match dress patterns. That is, to an extent, excellent advice: if you simply take the sleeves from one garment and pop them into another, they will not be a perfect match. This matters if you are making a smooth tailored garment that is going to be closely inspected and subjected to a reasonable amount of wear. But this is not the case for the average wedding dress and if you don't mind the odd little tuck or wrinkle where no one is going to look, or can cover a wobbly dart with a strip of lace, then use whatever patterns you have to hand. Remember that styles and fashions are constantly changing. The pattern companies match these trends so some of the patterns illustrated here may not feature in the latest pattern books.

The secret of good dressmaking is to enjoy yourself. If the thought of making your dress terrifies you, then don't do it. But if it tempts you, then have a go! Don't worry that you're only a beginner. Your local sewing and fabric shop will be pleased to offer you advice and encouragement if you chat your queries over with them. Alternatively you could contact the customer services department of the pattern companies. They are happy to give advice on using and choosing patterns and fabrics. You will find that there are many people who will be happy to help you create the dress of your dreams.

Just to show what I mean and to prove it can be done, let's look at some dresses that I have made recently, all from mix and match patterns. Not one was a straightforward reproduction of a shop-bought pattern. Each dress was made from a mixture of patterns or in unusual fabrics. Although they all look very different, they are similar in one respect: they are unique to the brides who wore them.

The eagle-eyed amongst you will spot that they use some of the same pattern pieces. This will show you, I hope, that you don't have to be too regimented about dressmaking and that it is possible to bend the rules and still produce lovely dresses.

Hand-made flowers and a pink sash were the genesis of the pink theme that was to run through Denise's wedding.

Denise's Dress

a simple matter to take the scissors to it and reduce it to a straight hem. She liked it, so we kept it. We added a pink velvet ribbon sash and the dress was just how she wanted it.

A first fitting for Denise showing the length of the train.

Denise wanted a plain dress; as a shy girl she was scared of being the centre of attention and didn't want anything too overstated. She picked the sort of dress she wanted by looking through catalogues and was determined to have white satin. I found a deep pre-gathered lace for the trim which we put all around the hem, across the bodice and around the veil.

Initially I made the gown with a train so she could see if she liked it. If she did not, it would be

Jackie's Dress

Jackie is a tall lady – not the image of a fluttery bride. This fact, combined with the knowledge that she was going to be married at a register office, convinced her she should wear a suit or a short dress. Nevertheless, I sent her a batch of designs and advised her to go on a tour of wedding shops and said: be sure, try on the whole works, just in case.

She rang back quickly. She'd found a dress that made her feel like a million dollars! It was long, it had a train, it was encrusted with lace and beading, and (you guessed) at a price of over a thousand pounds, it was well outside her budget! We set about reproducing the elements of the dress that pleased her, at a price that pleased her purse.

The ivory lace I used had a very definite pattern which I highlighted with beading – gold beads that looked particularly effective on the warm ivory satin. For a young lady who had started out anticipating a plain two-piece suit, she quickly warmed to the theatrical and demanded 'glitz', and lots of it. The headdress, which was made up in ivory and crystals, certainly reflected that theme!

Right: *The warm creamy satin of Jackie's dress is emphasised with beadwork in gold and pearls, and her bouquet is dotted with gold leaves and ribbons.*

Left: *Detail of the beadwork over the lace on Jackie's dress.*

Ruth's Dress

Ruth knew exactly the sort of style she wanted as she had tried lots of styles and found one that suited her. We had two extra factors to bear in mind: she was much better suited to having flesh showing rather than sheer fill-in fabric, and she wanted to use the skirt from her sister-in-law's wedding dress. The chance of using material from a dress that had started off such a happy marriage felt like a good omen.

The original had been an A-line dress fitted under the bust, with a short train. This converted very well to the bottom half of a waisted dress. Still whole, the skirt parts (a lining and sheer overskirt) were washed, ironed and shortened from the waist.

It was then a question of making a top, and for this I used an easy pattern that left her shoulders and most of her back bare. Ruth also wanted the back of her dress to shine – it was, after all, the view of the bride that most people in the church would see. For this reason we added a saucy bow with jewelled tails.

The front and, especially, the back of the bodice were covered with a wide lace that also trimmed the sleeves, hem and bow tails. This lace was then liberally embroidered with beads, pearls, bows and light-catching sequins.

Details of the back of Ruth's dress showing the beaded lace on the bodice and tails of the bow. The centre of the bow is a 'diamond'-studded belt buckle.

Carolyn's Dress

Carolyn's wedding was her second and she was very worried about what she should wear. My advice was to wear just what she fancied – to enjoy her day and indulge herself. She came back the following day with a packet of material she had been hoarding for ten years!

The story behind the material was unusual. She had worked with her new groom many years before when he gave a lift to her career and sent her off to India. Whilst she was there she bought a sari length of pure silk which was so beautiful

Carolyn in a dress created from two paper patterns. Note that she carries a matching purse.

Two paper patterns that held design features which were combined to create Carolyn's dress.

she didn't know what to do with it; so she put it aside for a special occasion. It was a lovely piece of material, it had links with her groom and she had been waiting for a special occasion to use it – I told her she couldn't use anything else.

She scoured pattern books for a style and came back with two she couldn't decide between, so I combined her favourite bits of both. We felt that in the end it echoed the sari style for which the material was originally intended.

Sandra's Dress

This is a bridesmaid's dress. Sandra was responsible for overseeing the making of her own dress as she lived miles from the bride. She gave me a sketch of the bride's own original gown and said the intention was to reflect it. Although completely different to either Denise's or Ruth's dresses, I used the very same pattern pieces. You can see what a different length, a different cloth and a different colour can do to create a whole new look.

Being Practical

I realise I have concentrated on describing fancy and traditional bridal gowns. In doing so I do not intend to neglect or ignore the bride who is looking for something more restrained. The advice I have given applies to all brides choosing any style of gown or dress.

If you are marrying in a register office and intend to make your own dress or suit, think carefully about it and don't fall into the trap of

Sandra's bridesmaid dress. Although it uses the same bodice pattern as Ruth's dress, it is very different. The stuffed cloth roll around the neckline is detachable and allows the dress to be worn at less formal occasions. The roll copies the design features of the bride's gown and is bound with a plait of dress fabric.

thinking that because you are working within a budget, or because you have decided against a church ceremony, you are forbidden from wearing something stunning.

Many brides want to wear something that can be used again, and I am all for this. But remember, it doesn't have to be a two-piece suit that will also be useful for work. It can be a smashing cocktail dress that you can wear at the firm's Christmas party! I am sure most women will get more pleasure (and further use) from a single posh frock, than any two-piece that they'll probably only wear to other weddings.

The reverse of this is also true. Just because you are marrying in church, it is not compulsory to wear a white dress with a cathedral length train and have five bridesmaids. There are no rules that say you cannot wear a tweed suit and brogues as a bride if that is your choice and your vicar agrees!

You may like to choose a short dress, even for a church wedding. Wear the style of dress that suits you and avoid the trap of going over the top into something long and flouncy just to match your traditionally-clad groom.

Don't be driven into doing the obvious. Be creative and be unique. It will be worth all the head-scratching, hard work and shoe leather just to have your groom begin his speech by saying how lovely you look and how proud he is of you.

A two-piece suit may be thought of as more suitable for a register office wedding, but it doesn't have to be plain or merely functional.

Left: These days dresses don't have to be white or ivory. This bride chose a lovely pink that suited her to perfection. Note that the heart shapes made of pearls in her headdress are repeated in her bouquet and echoed by the pearls around her neck. She wears no veil and it works very well.

Below: Some gowns say it all. Your choice of gown may set the style for your wedding, as here. Such a beautiful, elegant gown needs no veil, no fancy frills, no dazzling colour scheme. Opulent yet understated – for the bride who wants to make a statement without having to shout.

Chapter 4
Something Old, Something New . . .

'Can a maid forget her ornaments, or a Bride her attire?'
JEREMIAH 2.32

There are many traditions and expectations about what a bride should wear. Not many years ago, brides followed a rule of three:

A ring for true love
A brooch on her breast for purity of heart
And a garland on her head for joy.

♥ Nowadays we are more familiar with this little ditty:

Something old, Something new,
Something borrowed, Something blue.

And it is usually with our accessories that we follow the lead of thousands of other brides and choose items old, new, borrowed and blue to keep the superstition alive and our luck intact. We wear old earrings, a new dress, borrow a handkerchief from mum, and wear a blue garter.

But sometimes we forget that a few touches of imagination can lift us out of the ranks of the ordinary to one who truly has her own style. In this chapter I want to look at possible accessories and consider how we can use each item, whether it is to follow tradition, honour superstition or just look good! Accessories aren't just essentials that you have to wear, but instead are props to give you style and elegance. Think hard about your wedding style and your type of dress and consider whether you are making the very best use of your accessories.

Let's look first at what is often the most important accessory: the headdress.

Headdresses

The main points to bear in mind when choosing a headdress are these: it should flatter you, it should feel right, it should not fall off and it should not be a traffic hazard! It is also important that it fits the style you wish to adopt: a modern, two-piece suit could look a little odd with a tiara and 3-metre veil.

When you buy your dress, try a selection of headdresses and veils with it. Be prepared to try things that look unlikely or just plain silly. You may be surprised at how well they go together. I felt sure that I wanted a hat, but a fitting session very soon showed that I looked ridiculous in all of them and was best served by a headdress and veil, and a short veil at that. The opposite may be true for you.

There are traditional, simple, tiny, unusual and magnificent headdresses for sale or hire and if you find one that is 'you', snap it up! If you wish to create your own headdress, or have it made, that is another great option.

There are five basic styles of headdress: Alice bands, tiaras, circlets, combs and sprays. Each of these can be made using fresh flowers, silk flowers, plastic or fantasy flowers, feathers, ears of corn, lace or anything else you can think of!

If you make your own headdress there is no end to what you can include in its design. Craft shops, flower shops, gardening centres and cake shops all sell likely materials for creating a fancy headdress. You can experiment with colours, textures, shapes and finishes.

Headdresses can be white or ivory, can include a little of your chosen colour theme or be entirely composed of it. They can be matt finished or shiny. They can be static or they can be adorned with dangling, twinkling, swinging bits and bobs. The choice is endless – and the choice is yours.

Alice Bands

Alice bands are, of course, named after the little girl in the book *Alice's Adventures in Wonderland*. If your flower girls are dressed like Alice in Wonderland, then a simple charming Alice band is all that is needed to complete the look. A plain velvet Alice band or one of ruched white satin could look equally attractive on the right bride.

You can wire an Alice band together from scratch or simply decorate a pre-bought Alice band with flowers, leaves and ribbons to match your general style. You can vary the way you wear them, and the way you attach your veil, if you decide to have one.

An Alice band with white flowers, white satin leaves and crystal loops.

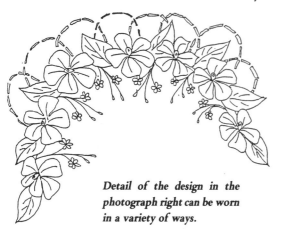

Detail of the design in the photograph right can be worn in a variety of ways.

Tiaras

I think tiaras are fun and have been somewhat undervalued in recent years. They were at their most popular in the 1950s and 1960s but their popularity faded a little during the 1970s.

A pearl and crystal tiara.

Design for a simple pearl tiara.

Now, I am glad to say, they have made a comeback because they can look really stunning with the right dress. Of course, we can't all have platinum or real diamonds, but we can have the *look* of them. Make your own tiara out of crystal beads, pearls and shiny silver or gold beads. Tiaras have a structure that begs you to experiment with drops and dangling pieces, so do so!

Tiaras can be worn alone to add a simple contrast to your stunning hairstyle, or they can be worn more traditionally with a double veil (see Veils).

Circlets

Circlets have recently enjoyed a revival and I suspect this was reaffirmed when the Duchess of York chose a lush fresh-flower headdress. Circlets are also extremely versatile. They can be worn high in the hair, they can sit on the back of the head or they can be pulled low over the forehead. Take care with this last style. I do feel that only the very good-looking can successfully carry it off.

Remember, if you intend to make your own headdress, dress your hair in the style you intend to wear, then measure your head. If you pile all your hair up on to your crown it could add a good few centimetres to the circumference of your head. Also, don't be tempted to make a circlet on the tight side to stop it wobbling: you may find

Silk flowers and a crystal bow form the basis of the design for this V-fronted circlet. Several ways of wearing circlets are illustrated.

Below: A satin circlet bound with pearls and beads with roses at the back.

that when you remove it later, you have a red band across your forehead.

Circlets don't have to be flowers wired together; they can be soft padded rolls of cloth decorated to complement your dress. If your headdresses have to travel far, consider this style as one which will not crush in transit. Even silk flowers can suffer harm when treated roughly.

Circlets can be worn on their own, with a veil falling from the back, or can be used to hold a veil over the head. I love this 'Madonna' look. It works really well for 1914 and later 'flapper' styles.

A design for a comb and various ways of wearing combs. Don't forget that you can wear more than one at a time.

Combs

Combs are generally simple to make and are popular for bridesmaids. I'm glad to say that the earlier fashion of adorning bridesmaids with a single large rose on the top of their head has gone. This was sometimes rather cruelly known as the 'miners' lamp'! Today's bridesmaids wear softer, more intricate and flattering combs. Remember too that combs don't have to be static: you can have flowers, greenery or ribbons trailing from them.

Rather than simply slotting a comb into your hairstyle, you can use it to create a hairstyle. Why not join two combs with strings of pearls or other beads and have an interesting decoration of pearls draped over your hair?

Combs are quick and easy to make and can have anything (well almost anything) stuck or wired on to them. Don't limit yourself to flowers, you can be inventive here. Why not make decorations from the dress material? Use it in simple pleats, rosettes or as bows. It will look very fetching and sophisticated.

Above: A spray of artificial flowers worn without a veil.
Right: A comb with everlasting flowers and pearls.

Sprays

Sprays are really just headdresses that don't have the specific structure of the other types. They can be used in a variety of ways and, since they are usually small and delicate, are particularly suited for the woman who wants her hair to shine and not a fancy concoction of silk flowers and tulle. Intricate plaits and rolls of hair are enhanced by the subtle positioning of a small spray of buds or ribbons. A spray may also be worth considering if you don't want to detract from the subtlety of your gown by overshadowing it with a fancy headdress and veil.

Wear your hair in a French pleat and place a spray down the fold. Lift your hair up and tuck a spray under the curls and over the hairpins. Wear a spray on one side of your head and let the end trail dramatically over one eye. Be adventurous.

Hats

Whether you buy or make a hat, consider whether it needs a veil, ribbons or trailing flowers to give it movement. A Juliet cap looks so much more romantic with a trailing veil, a Marie Antoinette flat-crowned hat looks wonderful with a mist of veiling tumbling from it and little pointed caps cry out for a torrent of frothy lace bristling out behind.

There is no doubt that sometimes we take such pains to fix a hat to our head that it begins to look rigid and unnatural. Allow your hat, or things upon it, to move.

If you decide to make a hat, or re-trim an old one, consider touring the junk shops and charity shops. Buy an old hat, strip it, and rebuild it to your fancy. Raid the jewellery counter in the same junk shop and use strings of beads, old brooches and medallions to decorate the hat. Borrow granny's cameo brooch or use one of dad's tie pins or cuff-links to give it a special look.

Did you realise that hats were once a symbol of rank? Whilst most of the populace wore hoods or caps, only the nobility, clergy or the very rich wore true hats (with a brim and crown). Women did not wear real hats until the sixteenth century. Bearing in mind that the hat is a relatively simple object, of a limited size range (it still has to fit the human head after all), there has been a remarkable

Every age had its own style. Capture the look of a certain age with the right sort of hat.

number of different styles. Every age had its own style and a mere glimpse of a hat can suggest a period of history as effectively as a whole chapter in a costume book.

I rather like the thought of a bride in a long, white riding cape with a white feathered tricorn hat, marrying a groom attired in true highwayman style. Let him wear a black cape, black tricorn hat and a black silk kerchief draped casually around his neck. Go the whole hog and furnish him with a mask and pistols and let him 'hold up' the guests for charity!

Hats that immediately capture a specific style are: Quaker bonnets, picture hats, berets, poke bonnets, straw boaters, bowler hats, cricketing caps, homburgs and trilbies. Riding hats (and here I mean the styles of the eighteenth or nineteenth centuries and not the pony club) and tricorns are a

very good example of what I mean. Choose a chic riding hat with a veil or feathers and you'll simply have to wear a dress styled on a riding habit and look absolutely ravishing too!

I yearn for the chance to design an outfit for a bride that will allow her to dress in a white top hat and carry a white, silver-handled cane!

As with headdresses, there are practical considerations to honour when choosing hats. The weather, how to fix them in place and whether they suit you are just three of them. How you wear your hair will also have a bearing. Remember that a neat little hat can do more to make your hair look good than three hours in the hairdressers.

Consider my illustrations and see what takes your fancy, then visit a department store and search for a shape that suits you.

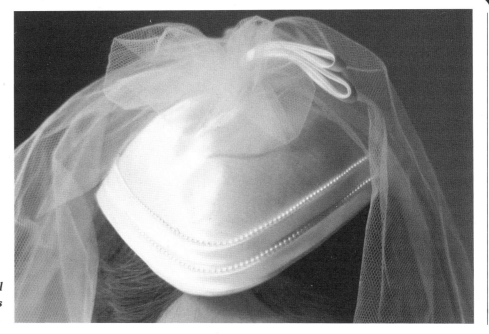

A hat in ivory satin with pearl trim. A short veil explodes from the top of the crown.

Veils

You may be surprised to learn that there are a host of superstitions, traditions and old wives' tales connected with wedding veils. An old bridal veil is thought to be luckier than a new one, particularly if it is borrowed from a woman who has a happy marriage. I'm all for this since I think that borrowing wedding regalia and sharing the luck and sentiment attendant upon them can make your own wedding day very special.

However, it is also said that it's unlucky to see oneself in the wedding veil too often and it should never be worn with the dress before the big day. Moreover, the veil should be the last thing donned before the wedding and the bride shouldn't see herself in a mirror until just before she leaves for the church. Well, that's bad news for most of us who spent ages in front of the mirror getting our hair and headdress to behave themselves!

Veils can be almost any shape or form but they can usually be described as long traditional; standard traditional; standard; short; and circlet. The traditional veils have a 'blusher', a second layer of veiling that is drawn over the face to hide

Opposite: Just part of the range of accessories that are available to the modern bride.

Above: A pretty parasol perfectly matches this lace-trimmed dress.

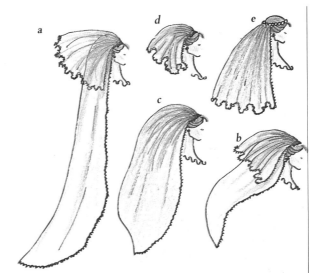

Common veil shapes: Long traditional with blusher (a); standard traditional (fingertip) with blusher (b); standard (fingertip length) (c); short (d) and circlet (e).

the bride's modesty. If you don't feel brave enough to concoct your own veil you can buy patterns for them.

Given that you can still see where you are going or that you do not crack a vertebra carrying its weight, a veil can be made of almost any material you choose. Good dressmaking shops will have a supply of net for veiling. Don't buy the cheap, stiff petticoat net as you will bristle like a hedgehog and deter your groom from coming anywhere near you! Instead, you should find the softer, denser veilings which are ideal for draping in soft folds and for offering misty glances to your groom.

You don't, as I said, have to use veiling; you can use patterned lace or chiffon if you wish. And don't forget that lace tablecloths, net curtains, granny's lace shawl or the petticoat from mum's wedding dress could all be used.

The five types of veil illustrated can be transformed into a choice of twenty-five when you consider that each could be made with one of the following five different edgings.

Oversewing

The simplest way to edge a veil is by machine oversewing. Whether the edge of your veil is straight, gently curved or cut into serpentine curves you can oversew the edge using a zig-zag stitch. Use white on white, cream on ivory or oversew with a coloured or metallic thread to add a little something. If your sewing machine doesn't have a zig-zag stitch, you can use an embroidery stitch such as buttonhole stitch to oversew round the edge.

Binding

Another simple method of edging is to sew lace or other trim around the edge. Satin or cotton bias binding folded over the edge and stitched in place will give a chic look that is quite different to a veil edged with lace. Alternatively, you can use a lace edging that matches your dress, or lace of any width to give different effects.

Bows

Sew or glue little bows at intervals around the edge of the veil. A packet of pre-tied bows can be bought for just a few pence and some come with tiny pearls stitched on to them. If bows aren't to your fancy you can use other motifs. A single metre of daisy trim will decorate an entire veil if you cut it into single motifs and attach them at intervals around the edge.

Diamante

Diamante or sequins can be glued at intervals around the edge of your veil. Scatter them over the body of the net so that you twinkle under the lights. If the veiling you use is up to the heat of an iron, you may even consider using motifs of iron-on diamante.

Beading

You can bead the edge of your veil to give it weight and movement. I illustrated some very simple edgings in Chapter 2. But don't overdo it with the beads: no one wants a veil that hangs like a plank from the back of their head! Think about using soft pastel-coloured pearls, silver, gold or clear glass beads.

Gloves

As with hats, gloves were once a sign of status. They weren't simply something to wear, they were props in civil or ecclesiastical ceremonies and day-to-day life. There was an entire 'language' constructed around the use of gloves: 'throwing down the gauntlet' in challenge, or slapping someone with a glove to initiate a duel,

are just two indicators of the role gloves once played. It was also customary to give gloves as a present or claim them as forfeit or favour (knights took a lady's glove into battle or tournament, not her handkerchief as is often thought). Moreover, gloves have been traditionally distributed as bridal favours at a wedding. Maybe that's something you'd like to think about.

The Queen wears gloves to protect her hands from the many hundreds of hands she must shake. I wore gloves to protect my guests from my perspiring palms! A warm, clammy hand may be a sign of a delightfully excited bride but it is not necessarily pleasant. We may choose to wear gloves for purely practical reasons such as these, but with the recent return of romanticism there are lots and lots of beautiful examples to choose from, so it becomes a pleasure.

Gloves come in all sorts of designs and fabrics: fingerless mittens, miser gloves, long gloves, short gloves, kid gloves, lace gloves and opera gloves. They are also very easy to personalise. If they are the sort that button at the wrist, simply changing the buttons will transform them. If they stop short at the wrist you can add a cuff using a lace that matches your dress. If there is detailing on the back you can embroider or bead this to make it extra special. If they are long gloves you can trim or decorate them both at the hand and above the elbow. Why not consider adding a fake diamond bracelet!

Remember that you don't simply have to buy gloves from the nearest department store; be adventurous. Go to jumble sales and see if you can find some Victorian opera gloves or pre-war hand-crocheted gloves. Go to boot sales and find a

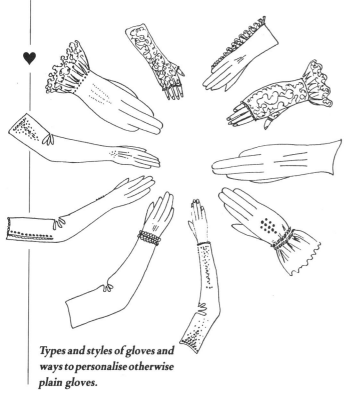

Types and styles of gloves and ways to personalise otherwise plain gloves.

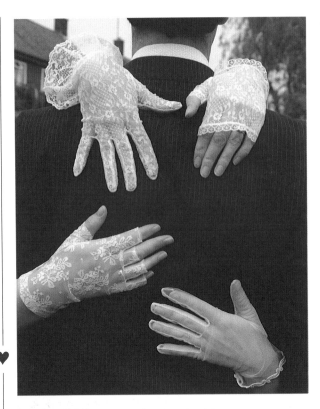

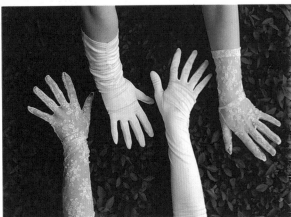

A selection of gloves (courtesy of Kirgloves) to show what is available for the modern bride.

bargain pair and learn their history from the previous owner. How nice it would be to wear gloves that a fond mother had worn to her daughter's wedding.

Bags

Of course, if you have to take your gloves off it might be useful to have a bag to put them in. There will also be no need for your mother or bridesmaid to carry your hankie, lipstick and compact if you carry your own bag or purse. Before you ransack your memory or wardrobe for a suitable repository for tissues and hairpins, let me remind you that wedding bags should be chic and pretty as well as practical. In short, your careful selection of an appropriate handbag can give you bags of style.

Your empire-style dress is hardly complete without a dolly-bag or reticule hanging from your wrist. Your smart 1940s suit is lost without a trim, leather clutch bag trapped under one arm. And how can you hope to emulate Nell Gwynn without carrying a basket of orange-coloured flowers? It can't be done!

There are, of course, customs and superstitions about bags: who would dream of giving a bag as a gift without putting a coin in it? Bags can also have sentiment. Carrying Great Aunt Emily's beaded 1930s evening bag, a gift from her fiancé, will not only please Emily, but will combine sentiment with your flapper style. Thumb through costume books or go to a portrait gallery or museum to see the right sort of bags for the period you have chosen.

Above: Carrying the right sort of bag can really add to your outfit.

Cloaks

Cloak is a rather broad term and I mean it to cover shawls, stoles, tippets, capes, boas, dominos and plaids – all the many variations that fashion and history have given us in the pursuit of elegance and warmth.

Cloaks have been made in every conceivable shape and material, and worn in every country by all ranks. They have answered all human needs, from warmth for the caveman who draped skins around himself, to the dictates of fashion such as

Below: Beading the backs of gloves is a simple way to add a touch of glamour to a plain pair of gloves.

the voluminous dominos worn at eighteenth-century masked balls.

Cloaks have been worn by both males and females so why not get your groom to wear an opera cloak? Then again, your attendants would look cute in fur-trimmed red velvet cloaks for a winter wedding. Continuing the idea of red, why not have a Little Red Riding Hood bridesmaid carrying a basket of goodies? Warmth and practicality can still go hand in hand with style.

Not every day is ideal for a wedding and you may need a cloak or shawl to keep out the freezing wind. If yours is a winter wedding, make the most of the possibilities. But don't let a cloak be a mere necessity: wearing a cloak or shawl will give instant style. Don a long, big-hooded cloak and imagine yourself as the French Lieutenant's Woman. Wear a white velvet cloak and become a Snow Queen or fairy princess. Wear tiny lacy drapes just around your shoulder and perfect the image of a shy Victorian miss.

If you want a nice lace shawl why not ask your mum if you can borrow the lace tablecloth? Stoles and boas can have a certain style outside the music hall but have to be worn with the right degree of carelessness. Just drape your feather boa or pure silk stole casually over your elbows. Perhaps you can let the ends trail dramatically as you slink up the aisle. Why not use most of a length of decorated sari silk? But take care – the famous dancer Isadora Duncan was killed by strangulation when the end of her scarf became knotted in the wheel of her car!

Don't forget furs. Few people these days would consider wearing real fur, but if you are trying for

A selection of cloaks and shawls.

a 1914-18 or a Veronica Lake look, then you cannot achieve it without a fake fox or ermine stole around your shoulders. Investigate the craft shops for fur fabric.

Underwear

My first piece of advice for a bride in terms of underwear is: BE COMFORTABLE. Everyone wants to look good on their wedding day, but many forget that they cannot achieve this without feeling good. You'll have so much to think about, you cannot afford to worry whether your seams are straight or if your garter is going to fall down. Wearing new sexy underwear will be no fun if the bra saws red weals into your shoulders or the suspender belt bites every time you move!

If you are happy in Marks and Spencer knickers and bra and know that nothing else fits satisfactorily, then wear them. Chain stores also sell fabulous wispy creations and designers offer us sheer, unadulterated temptation in silk. These days there are so many lovely, sexy, frilly undies available, it's a shame not to use the excuse of a special occasion to dress up (or down).

But modern, chain store smalls are not the last word in knickers. Why not make your own underwear? Pattern books include designs for all modern styles like teddies and camisoles, so you can make your own and include your own little touches. Let your underwear match your dress: matching lace, ribbon trim, embroidered roses can all echo your dress if you choose. Embroider monograms on all your lingerie and prove you wear your heart on your sleeve.

If you wish, you can go further and wear the right sort of undies for a particular style of dress. Find a period corset to suit your gown, or wear pantaloons if the style calls for it. Indeed, pantaloons may be something to consider if you know the weather is going to be cold.

I like the idea of a bride dressed in a rather puritanical, Quaker-style dress, while underneath she wears the most outrageous, sexy underwear; layer upon layer of frilly, silky petticoats. And only the bride and groom would know!

The modern bride is swamped with choice for pretty undies, but might like to consider underwear in the correct period style.

There are various items of underwear you can experiment with but I shall limit myself to discussing just three that you might like to pay particular attention to: garters, petticoats and stockings.

Garters

Garters are supposed to bring good luck and a bride's garters are more especially endowed with

Though the customs of snatching and tossing garters have faded, the custom of 'flashing' them has not.

good fortune. Historically, it was customary for the garter to be tossed and the guests to scramble for the honour and luck of catching it. Some guests could not wait for the garters to be tossed and so snatching them became common sport at weddings until the mid-nineteenth century. The lucky winners – yes two, for brides wore two garters – then wore them in their hats. More recent brides have photographs taken where she exposes her leg so that her groom or his best man can ogle her garter, so the custom has not quite died out.

Make your own garter from scraps of precious fabrics.

These days it is usually the garter where the modern bride wears her 'something blue'. Garters are no longer practical pieces of engineering; we wear them largely for show. I think garters are rather saucy but consider white, pale blue or pink garters to be pretty tame. I would prefer to see black, navy or red lace garters hidden under all that virgin white tulle. And so would your groom, I am sure!

Make your own garter out of snippets of ribbon and lace. Embroider your initials and attach suitably sentimental decoration – my garter was made for me by my sister-in-law, who attached silk flowers hoarded from her wedding.

Petticoats

Petticoats are an important garment for a bride. You can enhance or destroy the style of a gown with your choice of petticoat. For example, it is senseless to buy a bustle-style dress and then wear it over a hooped petticoat. It is also pointless to wear a petticoat if the gown doesn't call for it, an underslip beneath some gowns may give more problems than style.

My illustrations show the sorts of petticoats you can use to enhance the shape of a gown. Indeed, some dresses depend upon the construction of the petticoat to create their particular style. Anyone who wants to emulate the 'Poldark' look of wide panniers will find it impossible without shaped petticoats, 'bum rolls' or hip supporters. Costume

Petticoats can make or break a gown: crinoline (a); bustle-style with 'sweepers' (b); a petticoat that is meant to be seen (c); a princess line petticoat (d); a small bustle (e); hip supporters or 'bum rolls' (f).

books are useful places to find drawings of petticoats and will show you how to achieve a bustle or supported train.

Don't forget that some petticoats are meant to be seen. Scoop up hems and fix them with bows and reveal the frothy, lacy glory of your petticoats!

Take care with hooped petticoats. I don't just refer to the fact that they are sometimes quite wayward and ultimately embarrassing. Remember that hooped petticoats make some dresses appear shorter; check this doesn't happen to yours. Occasionally I've seen brides wearing beautiful dresses over petticoats that have robbed the dress of all natural movement. Instead, she stands there like a bell-shaped tent and, with each tiny breeze, her dress tolls! This is not style.

♥ *Stockings*

Stockings have a vast array of superstitions attached to them. One of the commonest is that putting on odd socks or stockings is good luck. Why not go along with the theory and wear odd stockings? Under a long white gown, no one will see how you court good fortune. This may be especially useful if you can't make up your mind between all the fantastic stockings designed just for the wedding market. These days we can buy the sheerest stockings trimmed with bows, pearls, sequins, stars, anything at all in fact. Have a look in the shops and see what you can find.

'Flinging the stocking' was another wedding ritual. As soon as the married pair were put to bed by their attendants (thank goodness that custom has passed us by!), the attendants tossed the stockings over their shoulders. If they hit either the bride or groom it was a sure sign that the thrower would marry soon.

I have stressed that comfort on your wedding day is of prime importance. Bear this in mind in your choice of stockings. If it's cold you may prefer tights, even thick ribbed ones. If it is hot, then stockings may seem more suitable. If you just don't have the legs for stockings, or find suspender belts too agonising, then consider knee-high socks. These can be bought with similar wedding designs so you can still show a nicely turned ankle – just don't do the can-can! But, then again, why not?

Shoes

There is much luck, good and bad, associated with shoes. Shoes even have erotic overtones! Only consider how gentlemen used to drink champagne from ladies' slippers.

As with underwear, my rule for shoes is to BE COMFORTABLE. 'Wear in' new shoes by substituting them for your slippers at home for a week or two before the big day. If you don't have time to wear them in, and you know you'll have to walk on a marble or polished floor, at least make certain that you scuff the soles. New shoes are slippery.

Check the condition of the aisle at the church. Is it carpeted, does it have gratings? Be aware that you could get your heel stuck in a grating or threadbare carpet! Also, practise kneeling in your gown and shoes; you may find that your shoe heels tangle with your dress or hoop. Practise

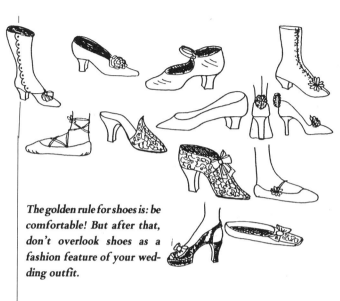

The golden rule for shoes is: be comfortable! But after that, don't overlook shoes as a fashion feature of your wedding outfit.

disentangling yourself or warn your groom that you may need his assistance to get up.

It's also worth checking your shoes for sabotage. It may not be a new joke but it's common for loving members of the family to write little messages (such as 'Help!') on the soles of the shoes of the bride or groom.

Short dresses just cry out for fancy shoes so do think about your feet carefully. Shoes, like any other accessory, have the power to make or break your chosen style. The careful selection of sandals, boots, slippers, mules, moccasins or espadrilles will have a lot to do with the attainment of a certain look.

Buy plain shoes and decorate them. If your craft skills are limited, concentrate on making just two shoe clips to brighten up the plain white court shoes that peep out from under your 1930s dress. Alternatively add buckles or big floppy bows if you want to emulate the musketeer look.

Jewellery

A wise bride will not overlook the importance of jewellery. The right suite of jewellery (tiara, necklace, earrings and maybe a bracelet or brooch) can add to your style.

Check portraits and costume books for the right fashion jewellery to reflect a period look. Your Greek or Roman inspired gown will look so much better when decorated with a copy of a period brooch and your arms will look less bare with bangles on your upper arms.

Of course, if your groom has given you a gift for the wedding, then you must wear it and style be damned. A lover's gift is more important than image.

Pearls and diamonds are common for brides, but don't be afraid of a colour in your jewels. Rubies, emeralds or sapphires can enhance a colour theme or simply break up the starkness of white.

Miscellaneous Accessories

There are many other accessories which can bespeak a style. Let's take a look at some of them.

Chokers

Anecdotal history tells us that the choker was invented by flighty young ladies in France. Their elders and betters told them not to let a man's hands go above their garter, so these dutiful misses wore their garters round their necks! Believe that if you will, but there is no doubt that chokers have a certain *je ne sais quoi*!

Consider a choker as part of your ensemble and exploit its saucy charm or simple elegance. Fashion plates of the ages will show the choker in constant use with all sorts of dress styles. A velvet band with a cameo clasp, three rows of pearls in a tight embrace around a long white neck, or a simple ribbon band with streamers reaching down the back to the hem, will all underline a particular style.

Chokers don't have to be black velvet; a simple length of baby ribbon tied with a bow is just as effective and much cheaper than a new necklace. If you like the idea of a choker, consider wearing your hair up to complete the elegant picture.

Below: Four bridesmaids with a clutch of accessories: parasols, dolly-bags and long evening coats.

Fans

Whether you want a closed fan, an open fan or one that does both, there are a variety to choose from. During Regency and Victorian times there was a regular 'language' of the fan whereby young ladies could flirt or convey messages without ever uttering a word. See if you can find a suitable list and include snippets in the speeches. Fans can be made of feathers, lace or paper. They can be theatrical, Victorian or oriental. What suits your style best?

Look through history books for ideas and identify the right sort of parasol or umbrella to complement your dress.

Whether they are feather, lace or paper; hand-made, shop-bought or heirlooms, fans are the perfect accessory for many brides.

Parasols

Parasols, sunshades or umbrellas can do a lot for a bride. They may even keep the sun out of her eyes and the rain off her hair. You cannot hope to emulate *My Fair Lady*, or *Hello Dolly* without carrying a parasol. Decorate them with flowers at the handle, at the point or around the rim. Don't forget, if you intend to open it up, that you can line or decorate the inside too! When you open your parasol, why not expose ribbons and bows, instead of a mess of ironwork?

You know your family: is it likely that they will sneak confetti into your parasol? You may want to check it's empty of confetti or rice before you open it. Then again, you may just want to ensure the photographer is watching when you do!

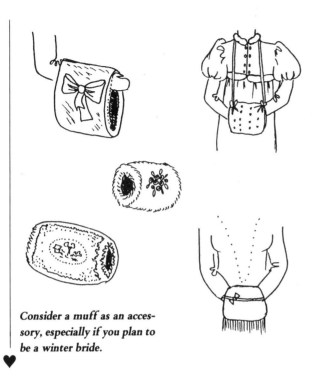

Consider a muff as an accessory, especially if you plan to be a winter bride.

you are dressed in a riding habit don't carry flowers; instead find a white leather riding whip. Silver-topped canes or shepherdess crooks, which convey completely different pictures, could also be considered.

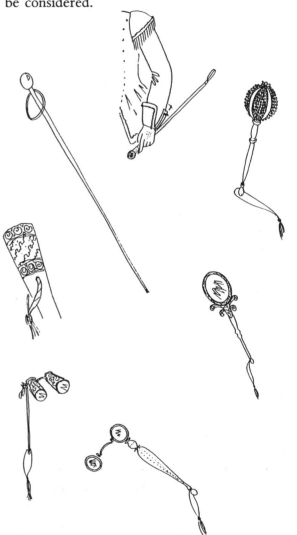

Muffs

A muff need not simply keep your hands warm, it can also be used for decoration. Moreover, a muff will help to convey a certain style: the 'Victorian Miss' look found on Quality Street tins, for example. Carry a huge fur muff for opulence, carry a dainty muff trimmed with lace and flowers for a coy look. Ensure that there is a pocket in your muff to take your purse, hankie and lipstick.

Canes

A cane or walking stick can be very useful for setting a style for either yourself or your groom. If

Consider walking canes or riding crops as accessories if it suits your style. Spectacles and other ocular instruments can become fashion accessories instead of necessities.

Spectacles

If you are likely to need your spectacles at some time during the day, to sign the register for example, then make sure you take them with you. Your bag or muff could be invaluable here. Also, consider making the prettiest of cases for your spectacles and hang it from ribbons at your waist in readiness.

I spent ages talking one young bride out of wearing her glasses. When I finally persuaded her to take them off I was appalled: her features simply disappeared. So we put them back on again. If you know you look better with glasses than without them, then don't be talked out of them and let vanity fool you into stumbling around like a mole in the sunshine.

Other ocular instruments you could carry to capture a style are opera glasses, a lorgnette or (very Beau Brummel!) a quizzing glass. Hang them at your waist from ribbons or fine silver chains.

Chatelaines

Chatelaine was a term commonly applied to a housekeeper or similar person. This is because they were in charge of the keys of the house and wore the chatelaine, which was a device or purse to hold them. It was usually hung from a belt at the waist. You too could carry a pretty little purse with keys or scissors, or hang a pomander, dance card or fan in this manner. If you want to emulate a truly Elizabethan style, make your own pomander, the sort that comes on a stick.

Some of the items I have suggested you hang from your waist could also be hung from your wrist. But take care that you don't get in a pickle during the ceremony. How awful it would be if your swinging fan knocked the ring right out of the groom's fingers!

Masks

A mask could be such a thrilling accessory. Whether you limit them to yourself and your groom or have all your attendants carrying masks, it will be sure to cause a stir. Carry the idea further and have a masked ball instead of a mere reception.

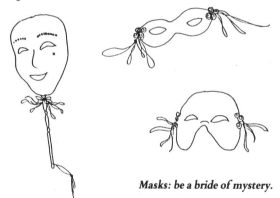

Masks: be a bride of mystery.

Handkerchiefs

A simple hankie may be the only accessory you need. If you just need to hold something to keep your hands busy, or if you feel that tears may be a likelihood, then carry a beautiful lace-edged hankie. Edge a pure cotton square (silk crumples in the face of tears) with the most precious lace you can find, or embroider your monogram in the corner. Use a hankie to replace your watchstrap or tuck it in your belt in a tumble of lovely lace.

Don't be afraid to cry at your own wedding and go well prepared for it. A bride's handkerchief is supposedly lucky and a bride's tears doubly so since they were thought to bring rain for crops. In some parts of the world it is thought that a crying bride will shed no more tears for the rest of her marriage, which is a nice thought!

In America it has become traditional for brides to embroider their initials and the date of their wedding on a lace-edged handkerchief, then pass it on to the next woman in the family to marry. This is a lovely little tradition you may wish to introduce to your family.

Perhaps a handkerchief is the only accessory you'll need. But don't crumple a tissue in your hand, carry a pure cotton square edged in hand-made lace as in this example made by Mrs Iris Martin.

Chapter 5
Beaus and Belles

'A happy bridesmaid makes a happy bride'.
TENNYSON

In all likelihood you'll find that there are more problems in choosing the attendants for your wedding than with any other part of the event. Every brother, sister, aunt, uncle, nephew and niece will wait in anticipation (or in dread) as you make your choice, and will not be afraid of making their feelings plain.

Throughout this book I have tried to encourage brides to be unique and inventive. But in this chapter my advice is to be kind to your attendants. Your fish-tail, skin-tight dress may look stunning on you, but a cerise coloured replica for your short, plump cousin will look anything but! Little imps such as younger brothers, no matter how angelic looking, will behave abominably if you force them to wear or do something they hate. Be original, but do think about the wishes of others and thereby make life easy on yourself.

Happy the bridesmaid, happy the bride. Think about what will make your attendants' day special. This is a perfect example of making similar styles suit both the sophisticated and the young: the flowers, the colours, the fabrics and lace, the hair — all perfectly complementary.

So, if there is all this fuss about choosing attendants, why do we bother? Well, if you get it right, your bridesmaids, pageboys, ushers and matrons of honour each have a very useful part to play in making your wedding special.

Historically, attendants at weddings served a very definite purpose. It was firmly believed that a groom and his bride were the prospective victims of every ogre, demon and portent of bad luck in the vicinity. Bridesmaids didn't carry flowers, they carried herbs, such as rue, rosemary or wild garlic, to chase off demons. In some parts of the world, brides still carry garlic for just this purpose.

Why do we sometimes have so many attendants? Having more than one attendant was done to confuse the bad luck demons. The theory was that if the spirits couldn't distinguish the happy couple from the guests then they could not put a spell on them. Indeed, this thought was taken further and attendants dressed like the bride and groom to give the local gremlins a real challenge! If you look through old photographs, you will find that you'll be hard pressed to identify the bride and groom from all the others. The idea of dressing bridesmaids in gowns similar to that of the bride is still alive, but it is now more of a fashion statement than a plan to thwart nasty demons!

Dressing the Bridesmaids

The subject of dresses for bridesmaids is often fraught with problems. Do discuss it with your girls and see what they might prefer. You'll have a lot of things to consider. Will they want a dress they can use again? What shapes are they? What sizes are they? What are their colourings? If you have a whole bevy of beautiful girls that range from blondes, through titian to brunettes, you will have to think seriously about what colours they can wear. Putting them all in pink just because it is your chosen colour theme will make you a lifelong enemy of your red-haired, erstwhile best friend. If you really don't want your attendants dressed in different colours, why not try different shades of your theme colour, or white with a minimum of coloured trim?

It is perhaps with the smallest bridesmaids that you can have most fun and be imaginative. Even in these days of Transformers, Thundercats and Terminators, princesses, fairies and angels still hold imaginative sway with little girls. Little boys may revolt at the thought of dressing up, but I suspect little girls will still jump at the chance.

I have illustrated a dozen simple styles for bridesmaids. If you consider that they can be made in at least two different materials (satin will give a vastly different effect to velvet, for example), then you can see we are immediately talking of twenty-four different styles. Take your choice from just four colours (white, pink, blue or lemon) and that's ninety-six different dresses from which to select. Is that choice enough for you?

What this means is that if another bride decides to copy one of the styles I describe, there is only a one in ninety-six chance she will pick the same style as you! That's on the way to being unique.

Almost all of the designs in my illustrations can be made from one basic dress pattern – 'Party Frock'. Have a look at the designs and see how varied one dress can become.

Designs for Bridesmaids' Dresses
Party Frock

This is a simple, waisted dress with puffed sleeves and a full gathered skirt. Items such as a collar, sash or frills are options. The style can be worn with or without a petticoat to give it fullness. It can be of any length from knee-length (for very little girls) to mid-calf (to show off pretty slippers) or floor length.

Red Riding Hood

Using a cape, with or without a hood, adds something to a very plain dress. 'Party Frock' will look completely different with a cape over it. Pop a basket on your flower girl's arm and she becomes Red Riding Hood. Alternatively, trim the cape with swansdown, and you have a mini Santa. If you choose a thin silk or satin dress, intended for later use at parties, a warmly lined cloak may allow her to wear it with impunity at your chilly March wedding. Another item to consider is an apron. Transform a plain dress by topping it off with a frilled and embroidered cotton apron.

Country Dancer

This is another very simple way to dress up a plain frock. Add a sash and allow it to trail over one shoulder. One normally sees this sort of ensemble as a white dress with a blue sash, but the sash can be any colour from the palest of pinks to the brightest of tartans. Why not have a white or ivory dress and add a sash of vivid tropical print to liven things up?

Party Frock, Red Riding Hood and Country Dancer.

Ballerina, Pierrette, Bo-Peep and Pantaloons.

Ballerina

This little outfit is simplicity itself. You could buy a pattern for it, but if you're really pressed, a simple satin tube with net gathered on to the elasticated waist will suffice. If you make sure you put a lining in the skirt you can use the cheapest and scratchiest sort of net without causing tears. Knit or buy a dancer's fluffy cardigan or bolero to be worn out of doors.

Pierrette

This style will probably look best on very little girls. Use a simple, long-sleeved dress and add large floppy frills at the neck and a few black pom-poms. Black and white looks best but you can change the colours to anything you fancy.

Bo-Peep/Cinderella

Bo-Peep is 'Party Frock' again but with a double layer skirt hitched into pretty flounces. Cotton prints and plain cottons will make your girls look the image of pretty shepherdesses, but silks and satins will turn them all into Cinderellas! As Bo-Peeps they should all carry flower-trimmed crooks; as Cinderellas, posies.

Pantaloons

This very obviously uses the 'Party Frock' pattern, but is transformed by the absence of a petticoat and the addition of little pantaloons. Use a rich colour silk for the dress and ivory or white for the pantaloons. Make a sash for the dress in white or

Above: This little bridesmaid needs no other accessory but her smile. See how pretty fingerless mittens are on little hands.

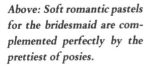

Above: Soft romantic pastels for the bridesmaid are complemented perfectly by the prettiest of posies.

Right: Black and red was a bold choice for bridesmaids but how beautifully it works, especially as they did not fall into the trap of over-doing the colours in the flowers. Instead they use light posies of pinks which soften the effect.

Roman, Calico Kate and Empire.

ivory. Pantaloons come in two styles, straight legged or those which are gathered at the ankle. See which style you prefer.

Roman

This dress hardly needs a pattern at all and can be made from two simple rectangles of material. There are, however, several good books on fancy dress costumes for children which will help you. Some pattern books have fancy dress sections; check them out. For this dress you really must use a soft cloth which readily falls into folds: thin cotton, muslin or silk or a fine jersey would be best. It is the trimming that makes this dress interesting. Choose simple ribbon, embroidered braid or upholstery cord to be different.

Calico Kate

This dress and pinafore uses a quite different pattern. It really works best with a high yoke and a six-panelled skirt. Remember that this can be made in two ways: a patterned underdress and a plain pinafore, or a plain underdress and a patterned pinafore. Why not have some girls one way, and some the other? Old-fashioned prints or fine dark needlecord look particularly pretty in this style. Try white muslin over black velvet: stunning.

Empire

This style of high-waisted dress can be made from the same pattern as 'Calico Kate'. The skirt, however, needs to be cut straight and gathered to

Celtic Dancer.

Maybe you can add a short cloak or shawl to trail from the shoulders.

Edwardian

This little dress may have to be made from a suitable pattern and there are several in the pattern books that would do. The style is one that is easy to emulate, however. Any straight dress which is trimmed with a low sash will be transformed. Originally, dresses like this were made in fine cotton and trimmed heavily with lace. You can do the same and create some stunning bridesmaids' outfits.

the yoke. This dress will benefit from being made in fine muslin or cotton with a rich ribbon trim to lift it out of the ordinary. Bonnets are an option for this style. If the day promises to be a little cool, top it off with a velvet spencer – a short jacket.

Celtic Dancer

This is 'Party Frock' again and is worn with a fancy waistcoat. Velvet is particularly suitable. The idea is to emulate Irish and Scottish country dancers. A pretty layered petticoat, a soft white satin skirt and black dancing pumps will complete the look.

Edwardian.

Themed Outfits for Older Bridesmaids

How can the above styles be transferred to older bridesmaids?

'Party Frock' can be easily transformed in several ways.

- Bring the neckline down to reveal a tantalising cleavage.

- Cut the neckline low then 'fill in' up to the neck with a sheer fabric in a subtle, complementary tone.

- Turn your attention to the back and lose most of it! Your girls will have a demure front, but when they turn around they will reveal deep V-shaped backs and plenty of pretty skin.

A beautiful bridesmaid. The gorgeous subtle colour of this shimmering dress is perfectly matched in the small bouquet and her circlet of flowers. But the one thing that makes her an example to be emulated is the exquisite fit of her dress.

Like little girls, big girls may well appreciate a cloak to keep out the chills.

Older girls can be ballerinas too, if you make the bodices more fitted and the skirts longer. Add soft chiffon sashes around the waist and let the ends fall on the skirt to give a real Pavlova style.

For 'Pierrette', dress your girls in white ballerina

Bridesmaids and pageboys aren't the limit on helpers. This attendant's outfit speaks for itself and demonstrates the affectionate spirit of fun enjoyed at this wedding.

costumes but add black velvet chokers and sashes and let them carry Harlequin masks.

'Bo-Peep' and 'Cinderella' can be achieved by using much the same dress style as above. Use a strapless, boned-bodiced dress (which they can wear again) and add false puff sleeves and little fancy gloves.

Unless they are really game, I would not dress older bridesmaids in pantaloons, but I would show a lot of frilly and flouncy petticoat.

The Roman dress will transfer easily to older girls and will be much enhanced by a bust to give it shape, and a stockinged leg peeping from a slit at the side. Let the folds on the back fall very low to reveal a pretty pair of shoulder blades.

Grown women look too twee in pinafores so don't copy the 'Calico Kate' look, just dress your girls in romantic styles in matching prints or opt for the slightly more risqué 'saloon girl' look.

The Empire style transfers well to adults, especially those who are happy with a low décolletage. Make the gown in fabrics such as muslin or silk which cling nicely to the thighs and give a feminine shape.

The low-waisted Edwardian look can be reproduced in any low-waisted dress. Perhaps it is as well to remember that low-waisted and straight dresses cover a multitude of bulging sins, so consider these styles for less-than-lean ladies.

Using your Bridesmaids

You will have to give some thought to how many bridesmaids you can have. You need not have any; there is no regulation that says you must do so. But if, for example, you marry in a church, you will have to make arrangements for your mother or a friend to perform the chief bridesmaid's duties, such as straightening your dress, lifting your veil and taking your bouquet.

Just as there is no lower limit on bridesmaids, there is no such thing as a maximum number. You could fill the church with beautiful bridesmaids if you wished, but you will probably find that natural limits come into force through your budget and common sense. Remember that they have to be dressed, trimmed, fed and entertained for the day.

The number of attendants, their sizes and ages will have a direct bearing on the form of the church procession. If you have a flower girl, she should go first to strew petals at your feet. If you have lots of little ones, you may like to 'herd' them with bigger girls at the front and rear. Alternatively you may just rank them behind you by height and hope for the best. Do be sure, however, that they know and have practised what they are expected to do.

It may be worth reminding you here that your girl friend does not have to be a bridesmaid in the traditional sense. She can be a supporter – a bit like a best man. Girls can even be ushers and undertake the relevant duties. You may like to consider dressing them in tails to match the principal men!

Dressing the Pageboys

Pageboys are not quite as common at weddings as bridesmaids. This is a bit of a pity, for some little boys are much more engaging, better behaved and eager to perform that a whole litter of girls!

You will have to bear in mind the character of your little boys when you consider their clothes. If they are the rough-and-tumble sort of scamps that beat up lesser brothers, they will probably scorn Little Lord Fauntleroy suits. If they are shy young men, they may dread being asked to wear something outrageous or even being part of the day.

These days one can hire or buy the most charming 'grown up' three-piece suits for little boys. One can even hire a pint-size top-hat and tails! Why not have all your menfolk in matching garb? Speak to your local dress hire company and see if it can be arranged.

But don't fall into the trap of thinking that your pageboys have to be dressed in grey or black. They can be every bit as colourful and cheerful as your bridesmaids. I have sketched a dozen boys' styles which range from the traditional to the unusual. I hope they spark off ideas of your own which reflect your interests and your wedding theme.

Designs for Pageboy Costumes

Traditional

This is really the basic pattern on which all the garments are based: it consists of a loose shirt and trousers. Use the bridesmaids' material for the pants and fake tie. Alternatively, if you are using a pale colour scheme, make the blouse from the material and buy or make toning trousers.

Fauntleroy

This is a fancier version of the 'Traditional' style. True Lord Fauntleroy suits are made in a rich fabric such as satin or velvet with a large lace collar. The top and trousers are usually the same colour with a toning sash or cummerbund and the trousers are nipped in at the calf as knickerbockers. Another favoured colour scheme is a white or ivory top with coloured pants.

Pierrot

This little clown uses the same items as above but the shirt is not tucked in. Add a couple of deep frills at the neck and pom-poms and dress your littlest chap as this tragic clown.

Soldier

This particular soldier is a sort of Hussar, but could be any type you fancy from a Grenadier Guard to a Beefeater. A simple jacket and pants can be trimmed in a number of ways to create different looks. Any uniform could be chosen, in fact. What is the little boy's current craze? The police, firemen, trains?

Sailor

Whether you opt for the traditional bell-bottomed 'Jack Tar' or a Victorian Midshipman with a straw boater, a sailor is a nice little uniform for a boy. If you give him a ship's whistle as a prop, save it until after the ceremony and you'll make his day – if not his mother's!

Traditional Fauntleroy, Pierrot, Soldier and Sailor.

Henley, Flamenco, Tails and Buttons.

Henley

If you've dressed your ladies all in white lace ready for a punting trip on the Thames, why not dress your lads in blazers and boaters? Deck-chair material or other striped furnishing fabric will be ideal to run up a little striped blazer.

Flamenco

A frilly shirt, a jacket cropped short and trousers made high at the waist will turn little Johnny into José the flamenco dancer. Hold up Johnny's trousers with braces and you won't have to worry too much about their fit. Why not pop your bridesmaids into flamenco dresses to complete the picture?

Tails

Lots of two-piece and three-piece suits are available in pageboy sizes and even, as illustrated, full dress suits with top hats. See what you can find in local hire shops, but personalise your chaps by dressing them in colour-themed shirts, ties and hankies.

Buttons

This is a neat little uniform that should be easy to copy. Buy cards of bright shiny buttons and adorn a plain jacket. Add epaulettes and your boy in a jacket becomes a busboy, a messenger, a panto Buttons, a footman. Let him act out his service role and carry the rings on a silver salver instead of a cushion.

Above: So proud in his grown-up clothes. His hat is big enough to drown in but he looks just super!

Left: Colourful casual street clothes topped off with bow ties make smart outfits for little urchins. I'm not sure about the bow and arrow though!

Above: Not all children are eager to perform for the camera. Here, this unhappy chap's blouse has the same pin-tuck detail as the bridesmaids' dresses and trousers which match their sashes.

Jockey, Kilt and Cowboy.

Jockey

This style is slightly unusual, but you may like to consider it if you have any equestrian links. It would also be a useful way of allowing a boy to wear the beautifully coloured silks your bridesmaids wear since a jockey's outfit is notoriously brightly coloured. This sort of outfit can even be made from remnant pieces of bright silks. White breeches, boots and a matching cap complete the picture.

Kilt

Whether you are Scottish or not there is no reason why you can't deck your lads out in highland dress. Velvet jackets, frills and sporrans finish off any kilt you buy (probably from the girls' department). Make your chaps feel more macho by letting them wear (blunt!) dirks or daggers in the tops of their socks.

Cowboy

Yes, this really is pandering to the little boy who won't wear anything else. But if your girls are dressed as 'Calico Kate', or your bigger girls are decked out as saloon girls, why not put little Johnny in a cowboy suit? A corduroy suit, maybe even denim or velvet, can be linked to the bridesmaids' costumes by using matching material in the shirt or neckerchief. Any old trousers can be turned into cowboy trousers by the liberal addition of upholstery fringing. Try it and see. Stetsons, sheriff's badges, guns and holsters can be considered if he needs that much enticing.

Older Male Attendants

You will probably find the room empties in a hurry if you suggest that older male attendants dress in unusual styles. And I wouldn't blame them! However, there is no reason for your men to be dressed entirely in suits that are black, charcoal, navy or grey. Or, indeed, in suits at all.

Three-piece suits are not *de rigeur*. Jackets and trousers are just as smart; blazers and slacks cannot be criticised. But don't limit yourself to such standard alternatives.

I know a lot of young men dread weddings because their mums insist that they 'smarten themselves up' and wear a suit. There is nothing quite so awful as a young man crammed into a suit when he is used to Levis and t-shirts. Have a look at some wedding photographs and you'll be able to spot all those in their first suit. They are the ones wearing sackcloth and ashes! They look every bit as uncomfortable and embarrassed as they thought they would. You want people to be happy at your wedding, especially if you have asked them to help out. They'll be much more useful to you if they are happy people!

Too many people add extra expense to the day by demanding that the menfolk turn out in new suits when it isn't strictly necessary. If it is likely to be a warm day, why not let the chaps just wear shirts and trousers? A new white shirt is much cheaper than a new jacket. If you want to make them match, ensure that they all wear the same tie, or give them a style by adding a silk waistcoat or cummerbund.

White trousers and shirts are very respectable – not even your most proper great aunt will be able to complain. You can adopt a whole style: add boaters and punting poles for the photos and you have the Henley look to perfection, whereas white plimsoles give an 'anyone for tennis' look. However, if you know they all belong to the local cricket team, why not persuade them to wear their cricketing whites? If your groom is part of the team, don't leave him out – put a new bat on the wedding list!

Most modern young men, however, are very dapper dressers and possess a wardrobe full of startling shirts and designer jackets. Check out their closets and see if they have anything suitable. Unstructured slub silk jackets which they normally wear to the disco can look just as smart if the worst of the creases are removed. They can all dress in the most different of jackets if they wear something to unite them in style. Give them their own type of buttonhole, for instance, or make sure they all wear the same shirt, tie or hat. Alternatively make sure they are fastened to the side of one of the bridesmaids.

Using your Pageboys

Pageboys are often included in weddings just to keep their mothers happy, rather than because they have a particular role to play. However, there are several duties that pageboys can undertake to make a wedding a little extra special.

Just as you ensure that the bridesmaids know what to do, make sure the pageboys are fully clued up as to what is expected of them. Spell it out clearly to little ones and get them to practise. Make a game of it.

You may wish to use a ring-bearer and it is usual for this to be a pageboy. I know that some people sew fake rings to the ring cushion and never allow the young ring-bearer near the real item (there is a lot to be said for making the best man wholly responsible for dealing with the rings). At the end of the ceremony, the ring cushion is simply turned over so that it looks as though the rings have been used. I find this sort of fakery a little excessive. If you are not using the ring-bearer, why have one? But I have to admit that only a fool would let little Jimmy carry the rings up the aisle on a slippery satin cushion. I would prefer to use Jimmy's cushion only when the rings are handed from the best man for presentation to the vicar. It's vital that they practise such a manoeuvre, for it's supposedly bad luck to drop a wedding ring, especially if it rolls away from the altar. (You just don't want to know what's supposed to happen if it rolls and stops on a gravestone in the aisle!)

In America a newer fashion is to have candle-lighters for late afternoon and evening weddings. Taking vows by candlelight is becoming ever more popular in the States and is already traditional in Germanic countries. It could be possible for you to use candle-lighters (or candle-bearers if the vicar doesn't like the idea) at your wedding and you could usefully employ older pageboys to do this.

Spend some time thinking about what you want the pageboys to do. If they don't have a specific task you might like to give them something to occupy their itchy fingers. Bridesmaids have posies that keep them occupied whereas pageboys are generally left empty-handed and available for

Your sisters and girlfriends don't have to be frilly bridesmaids; they can be ushers. This young lady was a perfect match for the top-hatted and tailed groom and ushers at this wedding. What a difference a skirt and stilettos makes!

Those that can claim title to a tartan can wear it and cut a dash.

With her marriage lines in one hand and a croquet mallet in the other, this bride soon convinces her groom whose rules they will play by! An unstaged 'snap' that captures the light-hearted mood that accompanied this friendly game. Take note of the bride's beautiful hair and headdress.

all sort of nose-picking devilment!

I have included some suggestions of things for pageboys to carry in the descriptions of the twelve designs, but it is not a definitive list. Think about your style or theme and see what it suggests. Do remember to be practical though. Obvious choices for Edwardian- or Victorian-dressed boys, for example, are a stick and hoop, a hobby-horse or spinning top. But would you want to let a six year old boy loose with any of those at your wedding? Similar considerations apply to little drums, trumpets or swords for tiny soldiers!

The Groom and the Best Man

Your groom is the one item at your wedding that you will have taken the most care choosing. Given that he is allowed out on his own, there is little more that most brides hope for than that he will be there, he will be sober, and he will be tidy.

In these days of dress hire, it is easy to dress up the groom and his best man in anything you choose. But for the bride who wants to emulate a society wedding I would add this: don't force him into tails if he is not going to be happy. Of course, if he wants to join in the fun, let him. You can be stunning together.

I have suggested in other chapters that you and your groom can be outrageous together, so why not adopt a 'Highwayman', 'Pirate' or 'Raffles' look? Be Anthony and Cleopatra, Andrew and Fergie, indeed anything! But remember, you'll have to live with the photographs for a long time. Don't do anything you may eventually regret.

A suit isn't the last word on your groom's attire. Think about his tie, a handkerchief in his pocket, his socks, his shirt, his waistcoat. My husband's best man fell in with my flame-colour theme by choosing to wear a peach tie, peach hankie and peach socks under his charcoal suit. I was delighted that he was so sporting. Mind you, he would have been happier in a black and peach short-sleeved shirt tucked into black jeans, but he was willing to please, bless him!

Of course, if your groom is in the Armed Forces or one of the Civilian Services he will probably need no urging to appear in full dress uniform. And if he is Scottish, it's only natural that he will appear in full highland regalia.

A groom is every bit as important as the bride; but that is something the bride and her family often tend to forget. It is his day too. Make sure he and his best man are happy with things. Seek their advice and ideas. They may surprise you with their inventiveness and willingness to help.

In most cases it seems it is the groom who is most nervous on the wedding day. Bear this in mind and don't do anything too outrageous for his sake. He should look forward to this special day, not dread it!

Enjoying your Attendants

'Happy the bridesmaid, happy the bride' is certainly true of most wedding days. One certain way to ensure that you are surrounded by happy and helpful attendants is to see that they enjoy themselves. Don't ask them to do things out of character, don't make them wear outrageous

Waiting for the bride. Three very different styles for these grooms but all of them look super.

clothes if they don't want to, and don't treat them like slaves. Instead, give them things to do because you want them to feel part of the event. Encourage them to enjoy themselves.

Why not consider using your attendants as a sort of cabaret or entertainment troupe if they are willing? Why should the best man be the only one to suffer agonies of nerves about making a speech? Use your attendants as a team. Get them to read telegrams, cards or make speeches. Why not get them to sing a song or act out a charade to start off the party atmosphere you wish to generate?

Often at weddings there is a 'dead time' between the official wedding breakfast and the start of an evening party. Use the attendants during that time. Why not match the ushers against the bridesmaids in party games? Consider quiz games or physical games like skittles, darts or passing the oranges! Of course, if your attendants are already dressed for a part, keep to your theme: have hobby-horse races or games of croquet to suit your Edwardian style.

There is, of course, another relevant old saying: 'never work with animals or children'. Depending on the ages and characters of your attendants, this may be the rule that you should obey. With some children it would be simpler just to let them be a way of introducing colour into your wedding and then return them to their parents when the photographs have been taken!

Above: The groom and his supporters discuss how to play a shot. An impromptu game, but an event that rounded off the day nicely — the bride and groom won!

Right: The best man with a key grip. Two- or three-piece lounge suits are smart enough for any wedding. I particularly like the red waistcoat.

Chapter 6
Floral Finishes

'And the Spring arose on the garden fair,
Like the spirit of Love felt everywhere;
And each flower and herb on Earth's dark breast
Rose from the dreams of its wintry rest.'

SHELLEY

In this chapter I want to talk about those items which are almost as much a part of a bride as her dress or any other accessory: her flowers. Most brides carry a bouquet or posy and it is a wonderful place to introduce colour, shape and scent into your special day.

A bride's flowers were originally herbs, such as rosemary or myrtle, and were chosen for their powers of protection and promise of fertility. Later, cut flowers and shrubs were substituted for herbs, although for a long time a preference remained for white flowers to symbolise purity and virginity.

It is interesting to note that many customs have long-established reasons behind them. We are all familiar with orange blossom and the modern substitutes such as philadelphus, but perhaps we are not familiar with the fact that orange blossom was only originally used because it came from an orange tree and oranges were widely used in love charms, aphrodisiacs and potions for fertility. We have to remember, oranges were only introduced in Britain during the reign of the Stuarts, so our preference for orange blossom is really an adoption of a foreign superstition.

Choosing Flowers

There are many flowers to use at a wedding and I have tried to list some of the most common and

Flower	Meaning
Bluebell	Constancy
Buttercup	Riches
Camellia	Perfect loveliness, gratitude
Carnation	Pure, deep love
Daisy	Share your feelings
Forget-me-not	Do not forget
Honeysuckle	Generous and devoted affection
Ivy	Fidelity
Jasmine	Grace, elegance
Jonquil	Affection returned
Lily	Purity
Lime	Conjugal bliss
Marigold	Sacred affection, constancy
Red Rose	I love you
Sweet Pea	Meeting
Violet	Faithfulness

colourful in this chapter. You will find charts on pages 132-6 giving a brief description of each flower or shrub and when it is available both in the shops and in the garden. I have also tried to indicate general colours.

Page 123 includes a brief list of virtues commonly ascribed to flowers and from this you may begin the process of deciding on those flowers you wish to use and those you wish to avoid.

There are some flowers, such as the lily, which always seem to be used for weddings. From ancient times the lily has symbolised purity and innocence and for this reason it has been used at funerals as well as weddings. In some parts of the country it is thought to be unlucky at weddings because of its associations with funerals.

Roses, too, are favourites at weddings. The rose has been a symbol of love for centuries, almost the whole world over. White roses symbolise platonic love and friendship and also silence, whilst red roses represent true romantic love.

According to tradition all roses were once white, but some became red by being stained with blood. Quite whose blood it was that performed the miracle is the subject of local superstition and debate, but the blood of Christ and other saints are legendary. The rose is, in Christian terms, a symbol for the Madonna and virginity. In earlier times a white rose was planted on the grave of a virgin and a red rose on that of someone who was noted for their goodness. There are legends of star-crossed lovers buried near each other upon whose graves rose briars were planted. As the years passed the briars grew towards each other and entwined, proof of the undying fidelity of those who lay beneath them.

Marigolds represent sacred affection, but one never seems to see a marigold used in a wedding bouquet or floral display. This is odd because the flower has definite links with things bridal. Marigolds are sometimes called summer's bride or husbandman's dial because they faithfully follow the sun, spreading their petals when it shines and closing them when the light is withdrawn. The flower supposedly symbolises constancy and enduring love and, historically, was often used in wedding garlands. Sadly it seems to have slipped from favour. I think it is time it was used again – especially as they are such jolly flowers.

We shall leave aside arguments of whether artificial or real flowers are preferable as each is suited to a different use, but it is worth considering exactly what you are going to use flowers for and how many you will require before you make this important decision. Your bouquet is unlikely to be the only floral decoration required for the day and you will want to consider your total needs before plumping for exotic orchids for everything. You should also give some thought as to whether you will carry flowers at all. Herbs, baubles, feathers and ribbons could all be alternatives to flowers in a bouquet. Indeed, these may be preferable if your bridesmaid or groom is subject to hay fever, or is rendered nauseous by the scent of hyacinths.

Consider the composition and colour of your bouquet before you put in an order. Will cerise flowers work against a blue dress? Is a white bouquet with green fern just lacking a little something in terms of imagination? Are you overlooking the fact that a particular flower is plentiful at the time of your wedding?

I, and the other bride who married in our church on the same day, shared the cost of the church flowers. We saved pounds simply because daffodils were plentiful in April; we bought bunches and bunches of them and just popped them into jars, vases and tubs in every corner of the church. In this way we needed only one or two special arrangements to be made up by the florist. The rest was very DIY but also very pretty!

The Bride's Flowers

Chances are that you will carry a bouquet and your bridesmaids will carry posies. There are many excellent books on choosing and making bridal bouquets and arranging wedding flowers in general, and I would suggest you pop down to the library and review these before visiting a florist or garden centre. Florists usually have a catalogue of styles and shapes to show you, but it is nice to take time to think about these things in the comfort of your own armchair rather than make up your mind in a busy shop.

If you are keen to follow the philosophy of the unique bride, you will need to think about ways of making your flowers personal to you. Anyone can have a yellow and white bouquet; it's what you put in it, and how you think of it that makes it special to you. Try and find flowers that have links with your birthday, star sign or name. Or choose flowers like those your mother or future mother-in-law carried. Find flowers that best match your colour theme, the time of year, or your budget. If I were to marry again, I would probably opt for some lily of the valley (the flower for my birth

sign) and daisies, since daisies are often known as margerites and Marguerite is the root name of Rita! Also, I am a cat lover and was pleased to find that daisies are sometimes known as cat's posy.

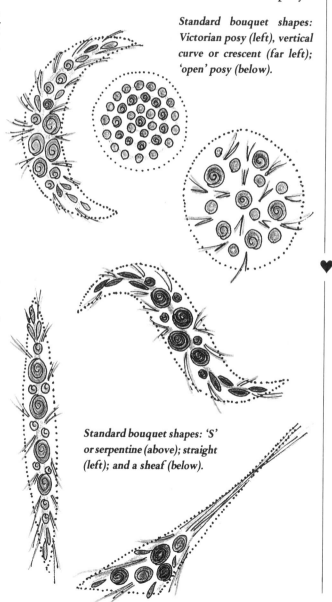

Standard bouquet shapes: Victorian posy (left), vertical curve or crescent (far left); 'open' posy (below).

Standard bouquet shapes: 'S' or serpentine (above); straight (left); and a sheaf (below).

Above: Near the top of the list of a bride's accessories must be her flowers.

Above: A stunning shower bouquet of fresh pink roses. This dexterous bride also carries a parasol.

Right: A simple yet romantic waterfall bouquet that perfectly complements this bride's elegant style.

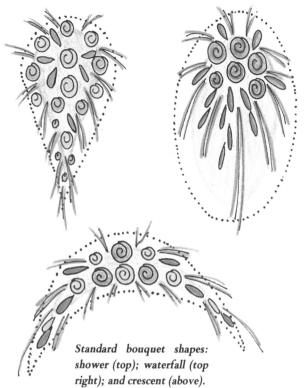

Standard bouquet shapes: shower (top); waterfall (top right); and crescent (above).

What a beautiful bridesmaid! She wears a circlet of dried flowers and carries a hoop trimmed to match. Remember to leave a gap in the flowers on a hoop so that your attendant can hold it.

If you can, make your bouquet personal to you. Choose your mother's favourite flowers, or use the same flowers as she or your grandmother had in their wedding bouquets. You could also think about using some flowers grown in your own garden, or that of someone close to you.

Don't forget to consider also what greenery or foliage you want, if any. You can use simple green leaves or ferns, or foliage that is white or grey. You can paint some leaves silver, white or gold to make them extra special. Make a few exotic flowers go further by padding out your arrangement with ribbons, feathers, ears of corn, dried flower heads such as cow parsley or honesty, ornamental grasses or even Christmas tree baubles.

Sometimes the simplest flowers work best: a simple sheaf of lilies, a single rose or a cloud of gypsophila can be stunning through understatement.

Another vitally important matter is the shape of your bouquet. It must be considered against your own shape when dressed in your wedding finery. How large a bouquet can you carry? Will a trailing bouquet tickle your knees if you have a short skirt or will a tiny posy get lost in all the frills of your dress? Can you use the shape of your bouquet to be different. I've illustrated the commonest shapes of bouquets. Perhaps you can utilise a shape to fit your theme: a curved bouquet will echo a rainbow or the letter 'C'; a shower shape could represent a kite or balloon. Perhaps you can use other initials? An 'S' shape is a fairly common shape for bridal bouquets, but Sarah Ferguson was also using it to echo the use of initials in the embroidery on her gown.

A Tussie Mussie

You don't have to carry a full-blown bouquet, you can opt for a posy or even a tussie mussie.

A tussie mussie is a nosegay made up of fresh or dried herbs and flowers clustered around a centre flower (traditionally a rose). The intention was to make the nosegay as sweet-smelling as possible. In the seventeenth and eighteenth centuries they were carried for their perfume as it was thought that this provided some protection against infection.

To make a tussie mussie, you will need 1 rose, 3 sprigs of rosemary, 3 sprigs of marjoram, 3 sprigs of angelica leaves, a doiley or circle of lace, an elastic band or sellotape (to bind the stems) and ribbons to decorate the tussie mussie. You could also use thyme, feverfew, lavender, mint or lemon geranium as aromatic alternatives.

Flower Decorations

You don't have to carry flowers in the conventional manner, you can carry them as decoration

Arrange three sprigs of three different types of aromatic plant around a rose and bind the stems together. Pass the stems through a hole in the centre of a doily and decorate the stems with ribbon and bows.

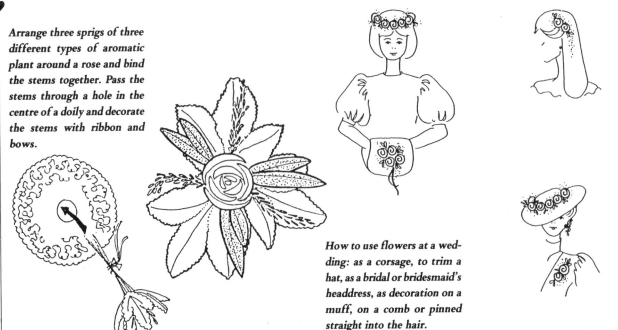

How to use flowers at a wedding: as a corsage, to trim a hat, as a bridal or bridesmaid's headdress, as decoration on a muff, on a comb or pinned straight into the hair.

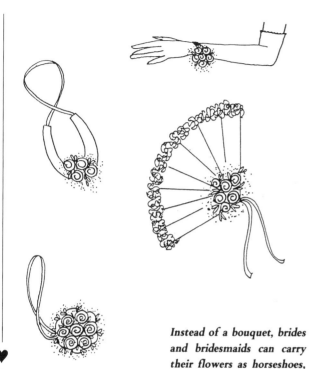

Flowers for the Participants

Other members of the wedding party may also wish to carry or wear flowers. Bridesmaids often carry bouquets similar to the bride, but usually smaller. You may prefer another style: flower baskets, posies, flowers in their hair or pinned to their dresses are attractive options.

The groom, best man, ushers and wedding party usually wear buttonholes or corsages. Before you opt for the traditional white carnations, think about your theme and colour scheme and look for something with more original style. Look at the illustrations and see what they suggest to you so that you can choose the best floral accessories for the wedding party.

Instead of a bouquet, brides and bridesmaids can carry their flowers as horseshoes, balls, fans or tiny posies strapped to their wrists.

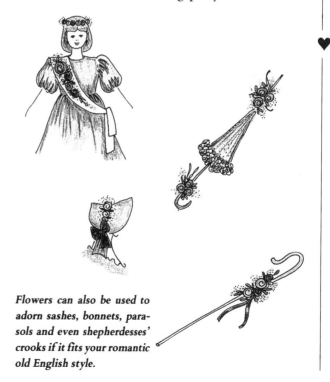

Flowers can also be used to adorn sashes, bonnets, parasols and even shepherdesses' crooks if it fits your romantic old English style.

on something else. Use them to adorn a parasol or fan. Decorate a mask or pomander with flowers and carry that. Wear flowers in your hair, on your dress or on a sash, wear a posy at your waist, dangle flowers at the ends of ribbons or strap a tiny posy to your wrist.

You could even re-introduce the bosom-bottle. In the 1800s, ladies used to wear posies of real flowers tucked into their cleavage. The flowers were kept alive by popping the ends into a little bottle filled with water. Dresses had pockets sewn into them to hold these little bottles for just such a purpose.

Artificial flowers were chosen for this bridesmaid. Her parasol is trimmed with large silk roses and single blooms are slipped in among her curls and ringlets.

Other Uses of Flowers

So where else, and how, can you use flowers? Here is a summary of some of the most common uses of flowers for a wedding. Think about the options and select what best suits your style.

At Home

You can decorate your home with flowers in many ways: on the front door; in tubs at the gate; in your father's car; in the house – especially where you may have your photograph taken.

I have seen one form of decoration that I think could be lovely for a wedding. Every year, in the market town of Spalding, Lincolnshire, they have a flower parade for which they build great colourful floats covered in tulip heads. Many people decorate their homes on the day of the parade by lacing flower heads into the hedging around their garden. Dark common privet looks simply stunning when decorated with bright pink tulip heads. If you don't like to dismember flowers in such a manner, perhaps you could use ribbons instead. Show the entire neighbourhood that you are celebrating!

At the Church

Churches look wonderful adorned with flowers. Think about placing them on the altar; in tall free-standing arrangements; on the altar steps; at pew ends; on window ledges; on the floor along the aisles; in hanging baskets; around and trailing down pillars; trailing from 'braziers'; at the lych gate; around the door; in tubs at the entrance.

Baskets filled with flowers, baskets trimmed with flowers, decorated bags and Bibles can all be carried instead of bouquets or posies.

Remember that at certain times of the year, the church is already well decorated with flowers for its own celebrations (Easter, Harvest Festival, etc.). Consider whether you can use this to your advantage. Contact the lady who organises the church flowers and see if you can arrange something that will be suitble for both you and the church.

At the Reception

Wherever you are holding your reception, you can enliven the scene with flowers: on the top table; on guests' tables; on the buffet table; on the cake table; on the cake; on the bar; and even in the loos.

Remember that many catering companies include flowers as part of their catering package. All you have to do is ensure that they know your colour theme.

Top: An arch of flowers over the church door welcomes the bride and guests.

Above: The simple addition of flower sprays at the pew ends makes this church seem very festive.

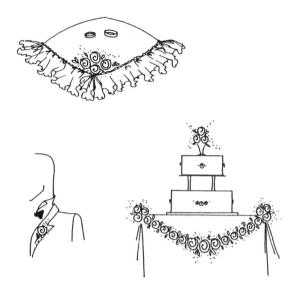

Decorate the ring cushion with fresh flowers or hang thick 'ropes' of flowers around the cake table to match the tiny posy in the crystal vase on top of the cake. Don't forget a very special button-hole for the groom.

Right: These flowers are particularly long-lasting and are almost always available as choices for your bouquet.

Long-Lasting Flowers

Name	Description	Colours
Alstroemeria (Peruvian lily)	Long stems of trumpet-shaped flowers.	Cream, peach salmon, yellow, bronze, orange, red.
Anthurium	Large, waxy, lily-like flowers.	Red, pink, white.
Carnation	Large feathery flower heads.	Many, but not blue unless dyed.
Chincherinchee	Flowers with stiff stems of starry white blooms.	White.
Chrysanthemum	Many varieties.	Many, but no blue.
Fern	Many varieties.	Green.
Freesia	Sweetly scented sprays of flowers.	Very many colours but missing true blue, red and pink.
Gladiolus	Several species including dwarf and long stems.	Many colours, plus a mauve-blue.
Heather	Evergreen shrub, thought to bring luck.	White, pink, mauve.
Iris	Soft, fragile blooms on long stems.	White, yellow and strong blue.
Ivy	Evergreen.	Dark and variegated.
Lily	Many species.	Many colours.
Lily of the valley	Delicate, sweet-scented bells on short stems.	White.
Orchid	Many species.	Various.
Rose	Many species, many scented.	All colours.
Stephanotis	Fragrant, waxy, star-shaped flowers.	White.
Strelitzia	Strong-stemmed flowers like a crested bird.	Orange overall but with touches of blue.

Availability of Flowers

This chart will give you some ideas on flowers to choose and when they are available. Florists will be able to give you more advice and suggest substitutes or alternatives.

In Shops												In Garden												Name	Description and Colour
J	F	M	A	M	J	J	A	S	O	N	D	J	F	M	A	M	J	J	A	S	O	N	D		
•	•	•	•																					**Mimosa**	Sweet-scented feathery yellow flower balls.
													•	•										**Jasmine**	Arching stems of sweet-scented yellow flowers. Winter shrub.
•	•											•	•	•	•	•								**Camellia**	Elegant white, pink and red blossoms with glossy foliage.
													•	•										**Hazel**	Catkins.
													•	•										**Alder**	Catkins.
•	•	•	•										•	•	•									**Forsythia**	Yellow flowering shrub.
•	•	•	•	•									•	•	•	•								**Narcissus**	Many varieties; white, cream, yellow/orange.
•	•	•	•											•	•	•								**Tulip**	Some double peony types; most colours but not true blue.
•	•	•	•											•	•	•								**Hyacinth**	Sweet-scented. White, blue, pink and cream. Single flowers can be wired for bouquets.
														•	•	•								**Currant (flowering)**	Pink flower clusters.
															•									**Amelanchier**	Pure white star-shaped flowers.
															•									**Damson/Plum**	Fruit blossom. Starry white sprays.
															•									**Acer**	Bright green flowers appear before leaves.
															•	•								**Spirea**	Shrub with clusters of white flowers along the stems. One variety is called bridal wreath.
															•	•								**Broom**	White, cream, peach, yellow or flame pea-shaped flowers.

In Shops												In Garden												Name	Description and Colour
J	F	M	A	M	J	J	A	S	O	N	D	J	F	M	A	M	J	J	A	S	O	N	D		
																•	•	•	•	•	•	•		**Clematis**	White and all tints through to purple.
				•	•												•	•	•	•	•			**Allium**	Many sizes and colours. Largest heads of flowers in pink to mauve range; some white and yellow.
•	•	•	•													•	•							**Lilac**	White, mauve to purple trailing flower clusters. Scented.
		•	•	•	•	•											•	•	•	•				**Antirrhinum**	Rich colours including white, pink, peach, cream and deepest ruby red.
		•	•	•													•	•	•	•				**Astilbe**	Plume-like heads of small flowers which give a cloud effect. White, cream, pink.
		•	•	•	•	•											•	•	•	•				**Sweet pea**	Soft, pastel papery flowers.
		•	•	•	•	•											•	•	•	•				**Stock**	Sweet-scented. Mauve, cream, pinks, white.
		•	•	•	•	•	•	•									•	•	•	•	•			**Hydrangea**	White, blues, pinks. Autumn turns flower heads to subtle tones.
																•								**Pear**	White blossom.
		•														•								**Crab apple**	Freely borne blossom in white, pink or crimson.
																•								**Apple**	Pink blossom buds open to white flowers.
																•	•							**Cow parsley**	Wild plant. White feathery heads of flowers. Dries well.
																•	•	•	•	•	•			**Artemesia**	Feathery grey-leaved foliage.
			•	•														•	•	•	•			**Cornflower**	Blue feathery flower; pink and white available.
																•	•	•	•					**Foxglove**	Pink and white are common. Tall elegant spike of bell-shaped flowers.
			•	•	•												•	•	•	•				**Campanula**	Bell-shaped white and blue flowers. Long trailing stems.

	In Shops												In Garden												Name	Description and Colour
	J	F	M	A	M	J	J	A	S	O	N	D	J	F	M	A	M	J	J	A	S	O	N	D		
				•	•	•												•	•	•	•	•			**Delphinium**	Tall blue flower spike. Also white varieties.
				•	•	•	•											•	•	•				**Phlox**	Scented heads of blooms. White, soft pinks, mauves and purples.
				•	•	•	•	•	•	•								•	•	•	•			**Scabious**	Soft blue, dome-shaped flower heads.
						•	•									•	•	•						**Peony**	Large, satiny textured flowers. White to deep red.
																		•						**Buddleia**	Arching branches with lavender-blue flower spikes.
																		•	•					**Aruncus**	Tall, feathery, cream plumes of flowers.
						•	•											•	•					**Sweet william**	Large, bright coloured flower heads on stiff stems. Many and variegated colours.
						•												•	•	•				**Lupin**	Tall columnar flower with wide colour range including white and cream.
						•	•											•	•	•				**Philadelphus**	White blossom-like scented shrub (mock orange).
						•	•	•										•	•	•				**Foxtail lily**	Tall spikes of white, cream, peach, pink and yellow star-shaped flowers.
																		•	•	•				**Nepeta (catmint)**	Delicate grey foliage and small blue flowers.
						•	•	•	•									•	•	•	•			**Gypsophilia**	Small fussy white flowers, gives good cloud effects.
																		•	•	•	•			**Love lies bleeding**	Flower heads droop from long stems.
																		•	•	•	•	•		**Rose**	Shrub, rambler, floribunda, hybrid tea and climbing varieties. All colours, some scented.
																		•						**Lime**	Tree. Interesting foliage.
							•	•	•									•	•	•				**Lavender**	Blue, scented spikes with fine grey foliage.

In Shops												In Garden												Name	Description and Colour
J	F	M	A	M	J	J	A	S	O	N	D	J	F	M	A	M	J	J	A	S	O	N	D		
						•	•	•											•	•	•			**Nicotiana**	White and some shades. Sweet scented trumpets. Tobacco plant.
					•	•	•												•	•				**Larkspur**	Annual delphinium in shades of blue and pink.
						•	•	•	•										•	•	•	•		**Dahlia**	Many petal shapes and sizes. Vibrant colours and soft hues, plus white. No blue.
						•	•	•											•	•	•			**Zinnia**	Colourful solitary blooms.
																		•	•	•	•			**Cotoneaster**	Shrub with red berries.
																		•	•	•	•			**Pyracantha**	Shrub, thorny, bears orange shiny berries.
							•	•										•	•	•	•			**Symphoricarpos**	Graceful curving branches of white berries.
Evergreen																								**Vinca**	Good trailing foliage.
Evergreen																								**Viburnum**	Shrub with attractive foliage. Pinkish white flowers Nov-Mar.

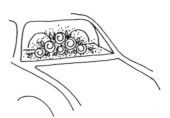

Don't forget to decorate your house with garlands over the door, or wind ribbons and sprays in and out of the stairs and lastly, put flowers in the car.

Chapter 7
Enjoying the Big Day

'I sing of brooks, of blossoms, birds and bowers
Of April, May, of June and July flowers
I sing of May-poles, hockcarts, wassails, wakes
Of Bridegrooms, Brides and of their bridal cakes . . .'

ROBERT HERRICK

All weddings begin with a proposal of one kind or another. These, due to human nature, range through the romantic and practical right down to the just plain silly. I can boast of a delightfully romantic proposal which heralded a fairly short but happy engagement. My husband treated me to a weekend in Paris and then proposed at midnight on a bridge over the Seine, with Notre Dame Cathedral lit up behind us like a fairy castle. It was splendid! Newly engaged couples are usually happy, sure in their love and glowing with pride. Latterly, engaged couples are typically miserable, haggard and at each other's throats with the worry and nervousness that comes with the approach of the wedding. You just have to remind yourself why you are doing it. There is really only one answer: you are in love.

Choosing Rings

For the romantic, the engagement and the purchase of the engagement ring is the first opportunity to let sentiment and family history creep in. The modern notion of an engagement ring is a solitaire diamond, but this is really a fairly new development. For the Victorians it was a ring set with stones, similar to our eternity rings, and before that, engagement rings were simply plain bands. Sometimes there were two rings, one worn by the woman and one by the man. At the wedding the two rings were brought together and united to form the bride's wedding ring.

It is not uncommon for couples to choose a ring set with coloured semi-precious stones. Prince Andrew designed a ruby and diamond ring for his fiancée, whilst Lady Diana Spencer opted for a sapphire and diamond ring for her betrothal ring. It's a good time to check up on what your birthstone is and remember that a fiancé's birthstone is said to be especially lucky in an engagement ring.

I was surprised to discover that all styles of rings did not suit all hands. I tried on just about the entire stock of emeralds in the shops in my home town and most looked quite out of place on my finger. So whilst it is a romantic notion that your fiancé should buy a ring and offer it to you at the moment of the proposal, do drop a few hints about what would suit you. Quite the best way to go about the business is to choose together.

When you become engaged, people will give you gifts and cards. Do keep them. You will find later that wedding keepsake books invariably start with 'The Engagement'. The story is not complete without those first few days.

Invitations

Finding, choosing and ordering invitations and Orders of Service can be time consuming and tedious. Here, as elsewhere, the modern bride is swamped with choices. Walk into any card shop and you will find catalogues boasting dozens of styles and types. Alternatively, a glance through the bridal press will show you a host of companies that specialise in unusual or personalised products. And on top of all that you can even make your own!

If you really want your wedding to be stylish and unique, the first place to start is with the invitations. Let people know how you mean to go on.

Remember, invitations don't have to be gilt-edged cards with fancy script. They can be hand-written personal letters or pre-printed invitations where you fill in the gaps. In fact they can be any card of your choosing with your hand-written message inside: why not support a charity by purchasing their cards, finding ones to match your theme?

Of course, if your handwriting is not up to it, or you don't have the time but still want to be original, why not type your invitation on blank paper, have it copied (maybe even in colour on coloured paper) and slip that inside a blank card. Do the Orders of Service the same way and you have a matching set.

We designed an invitation that could be printed on a simple A4 sheet and folded to look more interesting. I photographed and then produced a drawing of the church as an illustration. You must know someone good at drawing who could do this for you if you don't feel up to it.

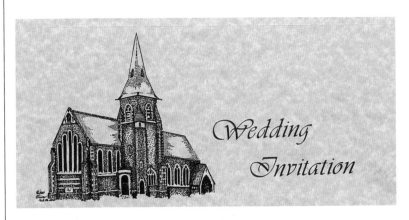

Above: A simple, home-made invitation.

Right: The photograph of 'our' church used to prepare a sketch for the invitations.

Invitations invariably depict doves, horseshoes, bows, ribbons or roses. But don't be constrained by tradition or what's in the shops. Remember your own style and theme and use them here: if you're copying a 1930s bride you must have art deco designs on stationery; if you're an Edwardian bride then opt for art nouveau.

Develop your caligraphy skills or beg a friend to use theirs to hand scribe a truly beautiful invitation and then have it copied at the printers. Experiment with layouts and styles before making a final decision. My illustrations show a variety of ways to play with the layout.

Choosing the wording for invitations is fraught with danger and is a happy hunting ground for arguments. There are formal and traditional ways of phrasing invitations and I have included some in this chapter as examples. However, I'm a bit against formality: in general we are sending this exciting news to friends, relatives and workmates. We would never speak to them in formal tones, so why do so in writing? Rather than: 'Janet and John request the pleasure of . . .' I would much rather see the more honest: 'Janet and John are getting married and would like you to help them celebrate'. These are invitations to witness something special. They are invitations to celebrate. They are not a summons to attend court!

But if you prefer a formal wedding and find it more comforting to follow traditional formats, do just that. There are endless books on the subject to help you get it right. For example, it is often quite

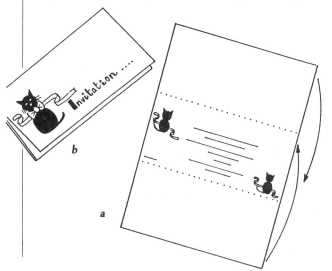

Left & above: A sheet of A4 paper can be folded twice to give a most attractive and yet simple-to-make invitation (a). When folded into a closed position, the invitation should show your motif and the word 'Invitation' on the front (b). Type your message of invitation in the middle of the three panels and decorate it with motifs (c).

It is nice, when the first fold is undone, to reveal the names of the bride and groom and the date of the wedding (d). To achieve this the paper must be printed double-sided as shown in illustrations (c) and (d). Note that one of the panels has to be 'upside down' for it to work.

difficult to get just the right wording to invite divorced parents to the wedding. Find out the correct way to do it and then see if you can live with it. If not, amend it to your own style.

If you do bandy traditional phraseology about, it's best to make sure you use it correctly. Little things make a lot of difference to those in the know. Requests for 'the honour of your presence' usually apply to a formal church wedding, whereas requests for 'the pleasure of your company' normally apply to a civil ceremony or invitation to a reception only. Either spell it out in plain English or use formality correctly to avoid confusing or misleading people.

Whatever style you choose, remember to include a reminder to respond. It doesn't matter whether you put 'RSVP', 'Please respond' or 'kindly respond', just hint that you need to know how many people will be coming. It's a good idea to put a reply-by date or your phone number to encourage them to act.

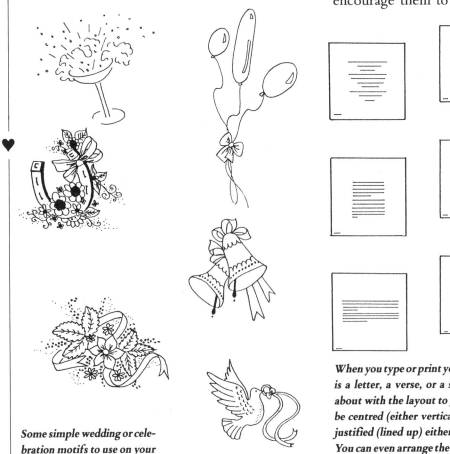

Some simple wedding or celebration motifs to use on your invitation.

When you type or print your invitation, and it doesn't matter if it is a letter, a verse, or a standard invitation card, you can play about with the layout to get different effects, Your message can be centred (either vertically or horizontally, or both), it can be justified (lined up) either to the left, the right or on both sides. You can even arrange the text to fit a shape: a zig zag, a triangle, a square or even (not illustrated) a heart!

In America they mark off special areas of seating, in the church or place of marriage, with ribbons or decorations. If you want to use your invitations to tell your grandmother you would like her to sit in state at the front of the church, or wish to include a best friend in the seats normally reserved for family, why not use the American phrase 'Please sit within the ribbons'? It's nice for them to know where to go, and it helps the ushers too. Of course, you've got to make sure that these reserved seats are decorated with ribbons!

Personally, I hate the 'us and them' divisions that occur between the bride's and groom's families. I also dislike the fact that relatives, even distant relatives the couple can't abide, are seated at the front whilst friends who have been the most supportive during the demands of planning the wedding are thrust to the back of the church. Decide how you want things and let the ushers, your guests, or both, know.

Another American notion is the rain-card. If an outdoor wedding or reception is planned, they enclose a rain-card giving alternative arrangements. You might like to think about this if you plan an al fresco reception.

Consider enclosing a simple map with the invitation along with details of public transport, hotels and places for pre-wedding lunches. It makes it seem as though you really want your guests to come. Also, decide at an early stage whether children are invited and, if so, be sure to mention them in the invitation.

But I'm stressing uniqueness, so why not do something really different. Print your invitations on balloons, or teddies and have them delivered. Why not send a singing telegram to a chosen few, put one big advert in the newspaper or have it written on Easter eggs or similar items.

Here we shall look at some standard ways of wording the invitations. But as I have indicated throughout this book, you can alter things as much as you like as long as it pleases you and does not confuse or offend others.

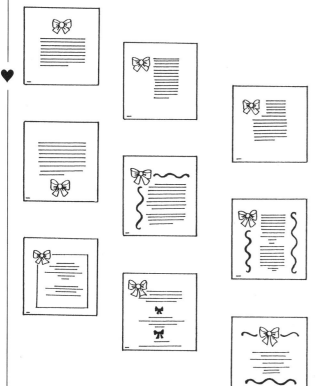

Left: If you have adopted a motif or image to be used throughout the wedding, don't forget to include it on the invitation. Here are some examples of how to position a motif to add a little more interest to your invitation.

When the bride's parents are the hosts, this is the most usual wording.

Mr and Mrs Joe Soap
request the pleasure of your company
at the marriage of their daughter
Mary Anne
to
Joseph Michael Public
Saturday, 7 June 1993
at 4 o'clock
St Mary's Church
Lower Sundon, Luton

RSVP

Mr and Mrs Joe Soap
request the pleasure of your company
at the marriage of their daughter
Mary Anne
to
Joseph Michael Public
Saturday, 7 June 1993
at 4 o'clock
St Mary's Church
Lower Sundon, Luton
and afterwards at
The Old Bull and Bush, Upper Sundon
RSVP

When guests are also invited to the reception afterwards the invitation is extended to include the relevant information.

For a service of blessing the invitations might read as follows:

Mr and Mrs Joe Public
request the pleasure of your company
at a Service of Blessing
following their marriage
at the Chapel, St Augustine's Boys' School
on Saturday 13 June 1996
at 3.00 p.m.
and afterwards at The New Hotel,
Anytown

RSVP

In the above examples, the name of the guest is written in the top left-hand corner, but it is becoming very popular to have this layout:

Mr and Mrs Joe Soap
request the pleasure of the company of
....
at the marriage of their daughter
Betsy Anne
to
Mr John Doe
at St Mary's Church, Upper Sundon
on Saturday, 13 August 1994
at 3 o'clock
and afterwards at
The Sundon Country Club
RSVP

Dear Mary,

Willy and Jenny are to be married at half past three on Saturday 17 June 1994, at St Mary's Church here in Lower Sundon. It will be a small wedding with a reception afterwards at our house. You know how much we would like you to be with us on that day. Please let us know that you can come.

Affectionately,

Abigail

For a small wedding to which only a few members of the family or close friends are invited, the above might be a suitable letter of invitation.

The honour of your presence is requested
at the marriage of
Miss Mary Lou Walters
with
Mr Wayne Dallas Jnr
at 11 o'clock
St Mary's Church, Lower Sundon
on Saturday 3 May 1994
and afterwards at
RSVP   *The Oil Barons Club*

When the bride and groom are the hosts for the wedding the format is a little different.

Willy and Jenny
are to be married at
St Mary's Church, Lower Sundon
at 3.00 p.m.
on Saturday 11 April 1995
and would be delighted if you would join them.

The ceremony will be followed by a party at
Luigi's Bistro

RSVP

If you find the traditional formats old-fashioned these two examples show less formal invitations.

Willy Smith and Jenny Brown
invite you to their wedding
at 3.00 p.m.
on Saturday 13 June 1995
at St Mary's Church, Lower Sundon
and afterwards at
Luigi's Bistro
RSVP

The Order of Service

Order of Service

PROCESSIONAL

Arrival of the Queen of Sheba   Handel

SETTING OF THE MASS: Missa Brevis in C   Mozart

KYRIE   Choir
GLORIA   Choir
EPISTLE

HYMN   Choir and Congregation

. . . .

. . . .

. . . .

. . . .

. . . .

. . . .

GOSPEL
ADDRESS   By the Revd. Henry Smith
MOTET   Oh taste and see how great the Lord is   Williams

THE MARRIAGE

OFFERTORY HYMN   Choir and Congregation

. . . .

. . . .

. . . .

. . . .

. . . .

. . . .

SANCTUS   Choir

BENEDICTUS   Choir

COMMUNION
Ave Verum Corpus   Choir
                                                    Mozart

SIGNING OF THE REGISTER
The Heavens are Telling   Choir
                                                    Haydn

RECESSIONAL
Sinfonia Cantata No 29
                                                    Bach

In general, the Order of Service for a Church of England service with communion is laid out as above.

Alternatively, a suitable format for a less formal church ceremony may be like the example on page 145. Here I have expanded the layout to cover four pages which fit nicely on a folded A4 sheet to be slipped inside an A5 blank card.

Marriage
of
Jane
with
Mr John Anthony Jones

* * *

Saturday 2 September 1993
at 3.00 p.m.

Arrival of the Queen of Sheba

Handel

Hymn

. . . .
. . . .
. . . .
. . . .
. . . .

* * *

THE MARRIAGE

* * *

BIBLE READING
1 Corinthians Chapter 13

Psalm

. . . .
. . . .
. . . .
. . . .
. . . .

* * *

THE PRAYERS AND BLESSING

* * *

Hymn

. . . .
. . . .
. . . .
. . . .
. . . .

. . . .

Jupiter - Bringer of Jollity

Holst

Wedding March

Mendelssohn

Where to Marry

In England one doesn't have too much choice about where to marry: a church or a register office are the only real options. Although parliament is considering changes to the law and will one day change the face of where and how we get married, at the moment we must content ourselves with what we have. In Scotland other rules apply and couples may marry at any time of day or in any place as long as the legal and civil requirements are met. If you are uncertain about any of the legal aspects of marriage, or of the form of a particular church service, or whether you have to be resident in an area for a certain period of time, don't be afraid to contact your local minister or the superintendant registrar at the local register's office; they will be able to help you. I have included details of helpful organisations in Chapter 8 to whom you may apply for further information, but your local contacts are always the best place to start.

It is possible to throw yourselves on the mercy of a vicar outside your own parish but be prepared not to be welcomed with open arms. This is what my husband and I had to do since we had no idea of exactly where we would be living during the months prior to our wedding and therefore, where our local parishes actually would be.

If you do not regularly attend church and yet still wish to have a church wedding, you must discuss it with the vicar. It is up to him whether he will allow you to marry in his church. He will certainly expect you to discuss the ceremony with him, and perhaps attend services at the church prior to the ceremony. He has no obligation to perform the ceremony if you are not a member of his church, so show respect for his office and his beliefs if you expect him to do the same for you.

At this point I would like to scotch the notion that all register office weddings are dull, quick and like a conveyor belt! It's not true. Ask around and find out about your local office and the people who officiate there. On the other hand, it's wise also to check out the churches and vicars too. I've been to some church weddings that had less soul than Sainsbury's! Find out what to expect and you won't be disappointed on the day.

It is important to get to know your vicar. After all, he has been to more weddings than you have ever dreamed of! If you have problems, or queries, he can probably help. Remember, he's seen it all before. He will want you to understand the ceremony and the nature of the commitment you are making to each other when you take your wedding vows, so he will be only too happy to answer your questions.

The Church Ceremony

There are many excellent books on etiquette that spell out the minutiae of wedding services and it is certainly worth reading these to find out what is expected of you and your wedding party. In general, however, you will probably find that you are offered a choice of three services. Obtain copies of the services and discuss their contents with your groom and the vicar. Remember, these are your vows – this is the very contract of your marriage. You have to want to say these words and you have to believe in what you are saying.

Everyone loves confetti, which is just as well for everyone gets showered with it. Check out the shops for 'ecologically sound' confetti.

There are three forms of marriage service in the Church of England. The oldest dates from the 1662 Book of Common Prayer and is less frequently used. More modern services date from the 1928 Prayer Book (re-published in 1966), which is similar to the 1662 version but with more modern language. The most recent form is from the Alternative Service Book of 1980 and both the language and the format have been modernised.

Whatever service you choose, whether you decide to include 'obey' in the vows or not, the basic form of the wedding is largely the same.

Here is a general outline of the 'standard' Church of England wedding ceremony. Other denominations differ slightly and you will want to find out the details from your minister. A wedding rehearsal is essential to put everyone at ease and helps to ensure that there are no surprises on the day. I am sure that most people are familiar with where people stand and what they have to do, but for the record here is a brief summary.

Who Does What and When?

The guests assemble at the church before the arrival of the bride. The ushers show them to their seats. The bride's mother sits on the front pew on the left hand side with close relations. Behind them sit friends of the bride.

The groom and the best man will have arrived early and be seated on the first pew on the right-hand side. The groom's close relations and friends sit behind him.

The bride arrives on the right arm of her father (or other male relative or friend). They are met by the vicar at the door and he walks them up the aisle (preceded by the choir if there is one).

At the altar, the groom stands to the right of the bride, her father stands to her left and the best man stands to the right of the groom.

The chief bridesmaid stands just behind the bride with the other attendants just behind her. The bride hands her bouquet, gloves or other accessories to the chief bridesmaid.

The minister starts the service with an introduction and prayer and goes on to ask if anyone knows of any reason why the marriage should not take place (always a moment of high tension as you worry about the practical jokers in your family!). The minister asks the couple if they are willing to make certain undertakings to love and care for each other.

When the vicar asks, 'Who gives this woman in marriage?' the bride's father gives his daughter's hand to the vicar who places it in the right hand of the groom.

The best man passes the rings to the vicar for blessing and then returns to his seat. The bride's father returns to his seat at the same time.

The vicar guides the couple through the vows and they each repeat the words after him as they exchange vows and rings. Try to control your nerves and speak clearly and confidently so that all your guests can hear.

The bride and groom then follow the minister to the altar for prayers, followed by the final blessing.

After the solemnisation of the marriage by the vicar, the bride, groom, best man, parents of the bridal couple and adult attendants move into the vestry for the signing of the register. After the signing, the recessional departure from the church takes place as illustrated on page 149.

The Register Office Ceremony

The bridal party should arrive in good time (about ten minutes early) and the guests not more than fifteen minutes before the time of the ceremony. Don't arrive too early as you are likely to get confused with the previous wedding. They do 'pack 'em in' at certain times of the year and at weekends. There is not much room to wait so it is better to time your arrival fairly accurately.

The bride and groom are called in first to have the proceedings explained and to pay the fees.

When everyone is gathered, the superintendant registrar gives a short address and then the bride and groom are guided through their vows. Although not a requirement for a legal service, the couple often then give and exchange rings. Finally, the bride and groom sign the register together with two chosen witnesses.

A Service of Blessing

Often, when people choose not to marry in a church or are forbidden from doing so (because one or other is divorced, say), they may like to have a small service of blessing immediately following (or a little after) the civil marriage ceremony. Also known as a Service of Prayer and Dedication, it takes place at the discretion of the minister and its format is often strictly shaped by the rules and preferences of the Bishop.

Carolyn and David (Carolyn's dress is described in Chapter 3), both entering a second marriage,

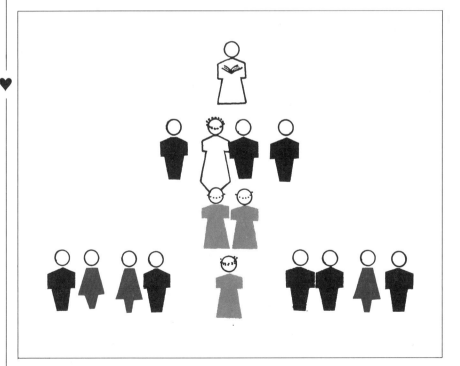

The bridal party and the beginning of the ceremony.

The bridal party leaving the church.

had a civil ceremony in the morning and then a Service of Prayer and Dedication in the afternoon at the Chapel of her son's boarding-school, which was a lovely and personal setting for them.

Such a service normally consists of a brief address, a reading, prayers and a blessing. Whether it is a low key affair or has a degree of ceremony is usually ruled by the minister, and this should be discussed with him. Some, for example, would not accept a bride in full white regalia or would not think it appropriate to have a full range of attendants, if any at all.

Choosing Music

Even though there is a proper and legal structure to a wedding, in and around it you can alter things to make a service that pleases you and is personal to you. It is, perhaps, in the music and readings that one can most easily personalise the day.

'If music be the food of Love, play on . . .'
Shakespeare

Your choice of music will help create a special mood within the church. Although you may find your choice is limited by the rules and wishes of the Vicar, you will be able to assert some personal choice. Get hold of a tape of wedding music and listen to it with your groom before choosing your favourites.

You can choose music to 'set the stage', because you like it, or simply because you know it would please your dad. Your reasons and your choice are up to you and your groom. Whether you have a piano, a church organ or a few friends playing guitars, there is no doubt that music adds a lot to the day. Why not opt for the more unusual and hire a Highland piper to pipe you into the church?

Music Before the Ceremony

While your guests are arriving and settling down it is nice to play calm and relaxing music. Your groom, too, may appreciate such balm to his nerves. It does not have to be religious music and can be ancient or modern. Discuss your choice with the organist well in advance, but here are a few suggestions to start you thinking along suitable lines.

'Water Music'	Handel
'Prelude, Air and Gavotte'	Wesley
'Nimrod'	Elgar
'Sheep May Safely Graze'	Bach

The Processional, the Entrance of the Bride

The processional should be something dramatic to set the stage for the entrance of the bride and her attendants. You want something bold to let the congregation know that now is the time to stop gossiping and pay attention. You cannot beat

'Here Comes the Bride' (Mendelssohn's Wedding March) as everyone recognises it, but there are plenty of alternatives.

'Entree Pontificale'	Bossi
'Pomp and Circumstance March'	Elgar
'Arrival of the Queen of Sheba'	Handel
'Trumpet Tune and Air'	Purcell
'Wedding March' from *A Midsummer Night's Dream*	Mendelssohn
'Carillon'	Murril
'Trumpet Tune'	Stanley
'Coronation March', 'Crown Imperial', 'Orb and Sceptre'	Walton
'Trumpet Voluntary'	Clarke

For each piece of music you choose, check (before they print the Order of Service) that the organist can play it, that the choir has heard of it and that the organ is up to it. What sounded

A highland piper may be just the thing to stir your Scottish blood.

magnificent for Princess Diana in St Paul's Cathedral will be less than terrific on your wheezy local church organ.

Hymns

There are traditional hymns for weddings (see list), but discuss the matter with your vicar and ask if he objects to alternative choices. Check that you and the organist agree on the tune to which each hymn will be played. There is nothing worse than launching into a hymn in your best voice, only to discover you are at odds with the organist! Perhaps there is something worse: when no one sings, because they have never heard the tune.

There are usually three hymns within the wedding ceremony though you and your vicar may have other preferences. Generally speaking, hymns are sung after the entrance of the bride; after the marriage and benediction; and after the prayers and final blessing.

It is worth choosing hymns that people know well or may enjoy singing. Men sometimes find hymn-singing difficult, so choose at least one loud and rousing hymn that they are likely to enjoy. Also, try to avoid the temptation of giving in to your sense of humour. 'Fight the Good Fight' is a great hymn, but you really should be taking this seriously! Here is a brief list of 'wedding' hymns.

'The King of Love my Shepherd is'
'Jerusalem'
'Love Divine All Loves Excelling'
'Praise My Soul, the King of Heaven'
'Dear Lord and Father of Mankind'

'Amazing Grace'
'Morning has Broken'
'Lord of the Dance'
'Lead us, Heavenly Father, Lead us'
'Immortal, Invisible, God only Wise'
'O Praise Ye the Lord!'
'Christ is Made the Sure Foundation'
'Glorious Things of Thee are Spoken'
'O Perfect Love, all Human Thought
    Transcending'

If the words of your hymns are to be printed in the Order of Service, check the front of the hymn book for details about copyright and then discuss the question of acknowledgement with the printer of your Order of Service.

Psalm

A psalm is usually sung after the marriage, but it has to be admitted that some congregations find them very hard to sing. It may be best to choose a well known psalm or leave it for the choir to perform alone. Hymn versions of well known psalms are: Psalm 23 – The Lord is My Shepherd; Psalm 121 – I Lift Up Mine Eyes; Psalm 150 – Praise God in His Holiness.

Signing of the Register

While you and the witnesses disappear into the vestry, it's common for music to be played to placate the rest of the congregation. Nowadays this is the time when many people play modern or popular tunes or get friends to play their own instruments. You may need a sound system and the permission of the vicar to do this. Remember your style here. If you have a truly Edwardian-style wedding, then 'We've Only Just Begun', sung by the Carpenters, is unlikely to be the most appropriate choice! You might like to consider something more traditional.

'Adagio in G minor'	Albinoni
'Choral Prelude'	Bach
'Nocturne' from *String Quartet*	Borodin
'Largo' from Symphony No 9	Dvorak

Leaving the Church

The grand finale, the recessional. Make it happy. Make it triumphant!

'Music for the Royal Fireworks'	Handel
'Wedding March' from *A Midsummer Night's Dream*	Mendelssohn
'Toccata' (Symphony No. 5)	Widor
'Prelude and Fugue in A'	Bach
'Trumpet Voluntary'	Clarke
'Triumphal March' Opus 53 no 3	Greig
'Grand March' from *Aida*	Verdi
'The Ride of the Valkyrie'	Wagner
'March Pontificale'	Widor

Choosing Readings

Readings are a good way to honour guests by inviting them to take part in the ceremony. Below is a brief list of references and suggestions for suitable readings. My husband and I chose not to have a religious reading as we are not regular church-goers and felt that it would be a little out of keeping. A friend we asked to give the reading found a lovely piece by Khalil Gibran. Try

Browning, Shakespeare or even pop lyrics as an alternative if your vicar is in agreement.

Biblical Readings

Love   I John 3:16; 4:7-19, John 15:9-17; I Corinthians 13; Song of Solomon 7:11-12, 8:6-7; Ephesians 5:1-2.

Husbands and wives   Proverbs 17, 20, 25-29, 31:10-13; Hosea 2:21-22; Ephesians 5:28-33; Ruth 1:16.

Marriage   Hebrews 13:4; Ecclesiastes 4:9-12; Matthew 19:4-6; Mark 10:6-9.

Praise and Joy   Psalm 8, 118:24, 150; Isiah 61:10-11; Jeremiah 33:10-11; Ecclesiastes 9:7-9.

Secular Readings

E.E. Cummings, Robert Frost, Kahlil Gibran, Shakespeare, Browning, Shelley, Betjemin and Christina Rossetti are all authors to consider.

Consider also song lyrics, words from plays or other inspirational prose. A dictionary of quotations is a good place to start: look up key words such as love, marriage, joy, bonds, vows and celebration and see how the famous used them in poetry and theatre.

Print the titles of works and the names of participants in the Order of Service. It helps your congregation to understand what's going on and just where they are in the ceremony. It also stops them asking each other 'What is that lovely poem/hymn/music?' during the service.

Special Guests

Children have special needs and it is no use pretending that they do not. If you just close your eyes, children do not go away, they just get louder.

Find out your vicar's views on noisy children. I've come across two quite differing views. One vicar stopped a ceremony and ordered the hapless mother of the squalling child from the church as no one could hear a thing. My own vicar felt that kids could scream the walls down; the ceremony was between him, the bride and groom and nothing beyond the altar steps had a bearing on it. Ask your vicar's views and drop hints to the parents of likely 'screamers' to save later embarrassment.

At the reception, consider whether it's worth separating the kids from the grown ups. See if there is a children's room available. If not, arrange for an entertainer, such as a magician or clown, or find a willing teenager to be in charge and organise games. Gifts, party-bags and special dishes (ice cream, jelly, chocolate novelties, etc) are nice treats and can all be held as hostage for good behaviour (for at least ten minutes!).

Consider other special guests and ensure there is adequate attention to their needs. Have you disabled or elderly relatives? Is there easy access to the church and the reception? Is there parking? Some guests have very special needs and you should think about them. Does the church or reception hall have an induction loop for the benefit of those with hearing aids? If it does, ensure it is switched on. Would large-print hymn sheets be better for guests with poor vision?

Think about these points: is there access for the florist, electricity or gas for the caterers, a telephone or somewhere to take the photographs? Whilst modern reception venues have excellent facilities, the same cannot necessarily be said of your home, the local scout hut or church hall.

Ask at the church if they can cordon off special areas for parking. It is common for them to put out notices if a wedding is due. Indeed, some even have white traffic cones decorated with ribbons. My rather morbid sense of humour was tickled to see similar black traffic cones stacked in the vestry for funerals!

Leaving the Church

Have you noticed how most brides and grooms seem to run from the church? It seems to be instinctive, but do give a thought to your friends in the congregation that are dying for the first picture of you as man and wife. Slow down and pause at the altar steps. Make sure your photographer intends to snap you as you come down the aisle. Most couples are beaming and it makes a wonderful photograph!

Your vicar will tell you the church rules about throwing confetti. Do abide by them and do use the kind that dissolves or can be eaten by birds. I love confetti and find it sad that some vicars have banned its use altogether but if you are sensitive to their reasoning, perhaps these bans will eventually be lifted.

Most people think throwing confetti is just for good luck, but do you realise it's really a wish for fertility? Originally, grains of wheat or other 'life-giving grains' were thrown over the happy couple

This isn't really intended as an example of desirable transport, but this scaled-down, working steam train is a perfect complement to their colour scheme.

Some people dislike red and white flower combinations at a wedding but here it is quite stunning. I also like the boldness of this bride in using red flowers as her headdress. She wasn't trapped into using wishy-washy whites or pastels and found something that was much better suited to her fair colouring. Other items to note are: her bouquet is curved, she carries a black cat for luck and her groom wears a stunning, matching red bow tie.

'Mix and match'! When you're in the building trade what else would you expect for a wedding present? These his and hers cement mixers were just a gag but they made the day memorable for the bride and groom.

Above: 1936 Triumph Dolomite — CVR Cars.

Above: 1951 Daimler Consort convertible — CVR cars.

to symbolise fertility and future growth. Later this was replaced by rice and then by the paper petals and cutouts we use today.

Why not be a little different and provide little bags of rice for your guests, or even birdseed, which are truly life-giving grains as the local wild-bird population will be only too pleased to confirm. However, throw seeds out on the street, not on a lawn, where they will result in weeds. Also, throw them high into the air so they fall gently over the happy couple rather than score a direct hit.

Cars and Carriages

There are as many ways of getting to and from the church as there are modes of transport. Consider walking, cycling, or riding on horses or in carriages or gigs. Other vehicles to consider are Rolls Royces, vintage cars, custom cars, balloons or helicopters. All are possible means of transport to and from the church or reception. Check your local press for what is available near you and check what cars your friends own. Why hire a white Rolls Royce if your boss drives one, and why hire a blue Granada if your dad owns one?

More and more companies are springing up, all eager to hire out gleaming white cars for weddings. However, bear this in mind: brides are invariably photographed against the car. A white dress against a white car does not always make for a good photograph, however good the photographer. If you wear white, make sure you have a blue or maroon car as contrast or interpose your groom between you and the white car.

The Reception

You will plan your reception to match your style, dreams and budget. Whether it is a sit-down meal with all the trimmings or a DIY running buffet, enjoy it. This is where you celebrate. If you are worried about the reception, if you are in agonies over the cost or dread the formalities of etiquette, cancel it! You've missed the point. You should be celebrating a marriage, not putting people through hoops of good behaviour.

Take time to circulate and speak to everyone. It would be nice if you and the wedding party introduced guests to each other – especially your parents to your friends. It might be nice to have a guest book for people to write good wishes in; perhaps you can take it around with you. You can go the whole hog and get one of the special 'bridal' quill pens for your guests to use.

The type of reception and the venue itself are certainly areas on which you can stamp your own style. A marquee will be quite different to a local pub, and an afternoon gathering different to an evening dance.

Your choice of food, wine and decor can all play a part in making the day special. For example, the wine we had for our toasts was made by my husband's father. Another labour of love was wrought by his mother who made our delicious wedding cake. They lived far from the scene of the wedding and were largely left out of all the fun and planning that went on, but in this way they really contributed to the day and we were rightly proud of them.

If you can't afford to spend the small fortune required for waitress service and full three-course sit-down meal, why not opt for a buffet? You can still offer a superb meal at a much more reasonable cost. Find a book on table decorations and let yourself be inspired. It can be done cheaply, it will just take a little time, that's all.

White paper serviettes are cheap but they needn't be dull if you have them folded in clever ways. Practice some of the special or traditional napkin folds. Some may even reflect your theme: the fan, the buffet pocket, the Bishop's hat, the crown.

Don't just let the food be for eating, make it stunning in appearance and save on the cost of centrepieces or floral displays for the table. If whole smoked salmons are out of your league, then don't forget that a tin of salmon goes a long way in a mousse and can be made to look magnificent!

Don't just serve a fruit salad, make it a centrepiece – display it in carved and decorated melons or hollowed pineapples. Don't just serve strawberries and cream, pile them up with sugar frosting into a magnificent display. Alternatively use piles of apples, peaches, grapes, raspberries, lemons and oranges to echo your chosen colour

Transport to and from the church is essential and many brides like to splash out and hire something a little out of the ordinary to make the day truly memorable. Whilst we can't have the likes of one of the royal coaches we can hire horse-drawn carriages or gigs. Some like to opt for vintage cars, but a modern miss may like something altogether more exciting and what could be better than a helicopter to whisk you away at the end of the day?

Cotton napkins in fancy folds. These designs can also be achieved with large paper napkins.

theme. Trim them with foliage and flowers (non-toxic, of course). Use what is cheap and plentiful at that time of year. In spring, have vast colourful spreads of fresh vegetable crudités with various dips; in summer, serve vast piles of (self-picked!) soft fruits and accompany them with silver dishes of whipped cream.

Alternatively, other non-perishable items can be used for display and decoration. Candles can be stunning decorations. Use them singly, in clusters of colour-themed beauty, or float them in bowls of water with flowers or petals. Consider placing bowls of pot pourri on each table as a centrepiece; they will also smell wonderful and later counteract the stuffiness of cigarette smoke.

If you can't afford fancy tablecloths or place mats, use wallpaper, wallpaper borders or doilies

to make inexpensive tablecloths and place mats that match your theme. Don't forget that bedsheets, valances and net curtains can be used in combination to make lovely, fancy tablecloths for buffet tables.

One can buy matchbooks, pre-printed napkins or napkin rings as keepsakes from many companies that sell stationery. They also sell scrolls which are usually a romantic poem, rolled as a scroll, slipped inside a 'gold' ring and left at each person's plate. This last idea is something that you can easily reproduce yourself – why not use a copy of the reading? Find out what is available in your area.

Many brides have adopted the eastern European tradition of distributing favours to the guests. These favours are usually pastries or little boxes of sweets. Sugared almonds are popular and, to many, represent the sweet and bitter in marriage. Companies that produce favours in chocolate, candy and sugar abound.

Of course, you don't have to buy favours; make or compile them yourself. Buy a packet of pipe cleaners and some artificial flowers and make everyone a napkin-ring to take home as a keepsake. Decorate the tables with bowls of jelly babies, jelly beans, liquorice comfits or Smarties; wrap them in scraps of net, doilies or wrapping paper. These little gifts don't have to be sweets; consider lavender sachets, pomanders, bath pearls, soaps or tiny posies. If you don't wish to pollute the venue with cigar smoke, give your gentlemen guests chocolate cigars! Another idea is to use party crackers to decorate each person's plate – a gift and decoration in one!

One way to impress your guests (and save money too) is to get a book on origami from the library and make little boxes to hold your gifts. Before you panic, these are actually very simple! Use brightly coloured wrapping paper and you will have gift boxes that can't be bought!

Continuing the theme of origami, you could use this paper-folding art to make place cards or menu holders. How lovely to have a flotilla of origami swans, penguins or lilies decorating the table as place cards – much more interesting than shop-bought cards. In any event, you really should make or design your own place cards to make the top table truly special.

Cookie or biscuit cutters are good objects to give you inspiration. Use a pastry-cutter with an ink pad to print simple bridal outlines (hearts, bells, horseshoes) on plain white cards. When dry, simply write your guests' names inside the outline and you'll have unusual and unique place cards.

Another European custom is 'paying for a dance' by pinning money to a bride's veil or dress. This is not such a good idea if your dress is hired,

Left: Place cards are easy to make. Cut out lots of hearts in red and white paper or card and fasten them together with red ribbon or cord. Write your guest's name in your best handwriting.

Fold an oblong of card in half lengthwise. Open it out and then, using a scalpel or craft knife, cut out a simple shape on one half taking your cut up to the fold. When the card is folded your shape will 'pop up'.

Buy plain cards and stick cut-outs from magazines or birthday cards on to them –leave enough space to print your guest's name.

Use cookie cutters or pastry cutters with an ink pad to print outlines on plain card. Write your guest's name neatly inside the outline.

A pink table setting. Favours of sugared almonds are displayed in hand-made gift boxes and paper cones. Doilies are used to give a 'romantic' feel to the table and the more romantic fan shape is used for the napkin. Compare this setting with the red setting below, although the same crockery and cutlery is used, the effect is quite different.

so why not make a white silk purse and collect your pin money in that? Let it match your dress. Why not do this as an alternative to the guests buying gifts or simply as a way to collect for charity?

At Jewish weddings, it is traditional for the groom to smash a glass. This is a symbol of the destruction of the temple in Jerusalem and a reminder of the beginnings of their faith and not at all associated with the European custom of smashing glasses after a toast. In some parts of the

A red and white table setting. Note that the colour-matched favours (liquorice comfits!) are displayed in origami gift boxes made from plain paper and wrapping papers. Also simple paper cones can be used and propped up in a wine glass. In the foreground more sweets (sugared almonds) are wrapped in tissue and scraps of net. The table napkin is set in a bishop's hat fold.

world it is traditional, at a bachelor party, for the groom to toast his fiancée, after which all the glasses are hurled into the grate so that they might never be used for a lesser purpose. I like this idea. Why not make arrangements for the best man to make such a toast to you and your groom? Before you start adding up the cost of such extravagance just gather all your family's old glasses together for a mammoth smash! How cavalier!

The Cake

The cake is an ancient feature of a marriage feast and symbolises fertility and good fortune. By tradition the cake should be as rich as possible to indicate abundance, but if you don't like rich fruit cake, don't have fruit cake. Remember though, that tiered cakes can't always be made with soft sponge, and soft-roll icing needs reinforcing too!

Wedding cake is lucky and there are country-wide customs of crumbling and hurling wedding cake to spread the good luck. The modern idea of sending cake through the post to people who were absent is not just a polite notion but a way of sharing in the luck of the cake.

Cakes can be original, special and witty. Bear in mind, however, the number of people you intend to feed. You'll not need three tiers for twenty people, nor will you successfully feed thirty people from a small chocolate log!

A good baker will be able to show you a range of styles, shapes and colours and I expect you'll be hard pressed to choose. But it's nice to have this sort of thing done by a friend when the sentiment

and care increases tenfold. However, if your cake-making friend lives in Edinburgh and you are marrying in Eastbourne, do give some thought to transporting it. Filigree icing and a nest of spun sugar will not travel well.

Whilst a wholly edible cake is nice, you will probably find that mums and grannies and aunts

Above: From 1935 we can still learn lessons about making a special cake. Here Ruby Moore gazes with evident pride and pleasure at the wedding cake which was made for her by one friend and decorated by another. A very special cake indeed.

Right: White trellis-work was the only decoration on each layer of this plain white cake, but on the top? An explosion of colour in an edible bouquet!

Below: A lesson in simplicity. A plain cake decorated with the tiniest of details in icing. Additional trimming of ribbons and feathers makes this cake a work of art. Horseshoe keepsakes are echoed in the motif on the side. The flowers on the cake are tiny corsages – what a lovely gift for special female relatives.

(and even you) will want a keepsake from the cake. Think about this and consider having just a few non-edible decorations to remove and give as keepsakes.

In America they have a groom's cake. Often this is scoffed at the bachelor party, but sometimes it is saved for the reception. If you want to be sure that you offer a choice of fruit cake or sponge, or marzipan versus no marzipan, or traditional cake versus the modern imports such as a croquembouche, why not instigate the custom of a second cake over here?

Continue your wedding theme on to your cake. I did this by duplicating my bouquet on top of the cake. You can colour cakes, shape cakes and trim cakes in a million different ways to echo your style or theme.

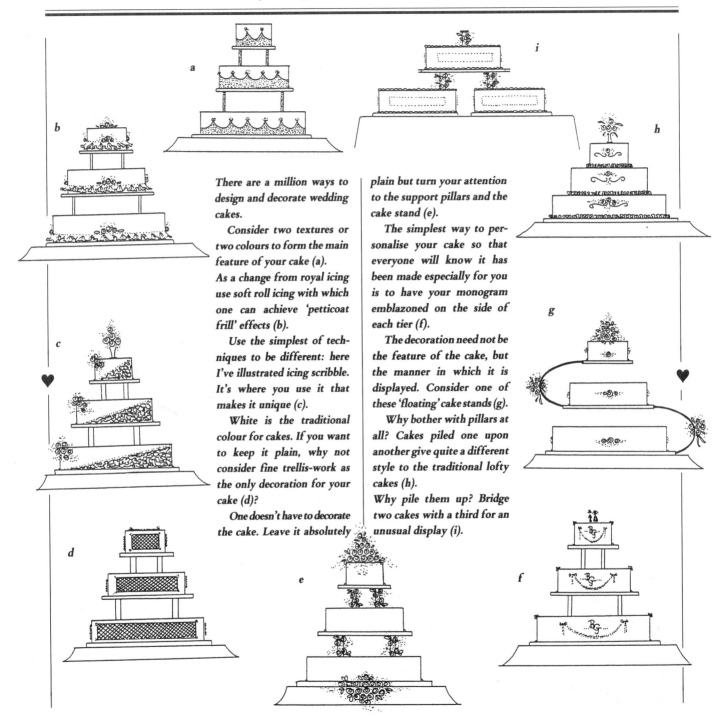

There are a million ways to design and decorate wedding cakes.

Consider two textures or two colours to form the main feature of your cake (a).

As a change from royal icing use soft roll icing with which one can achieve 'petticoat frill' effects (b).

Use the simplest of techniques to be different: here I've illustrated icing scribble. It's where you use it that makes it unique (c).

White is the traditional colour for cakes. If you want to keep it plain, why not consider fine trellis-work as the only decoration for your cake (d)?

One doesn't have to decorate the cake. Leave it absolutely plain but turn your attention to the support pillars and the cake stand (e).

The simplest way to personalise your cake so that everyone will know it has been made especially for you is to have your monogram emblazoned on the side of each tier (f).

The decoration need not be the feature of the cake, but the manner in which it is displayed. Consider one of these 'floating' cake stands (g).

Why bother with pillars at all? Cakes piled one upon another give quite a different style to the traditional lofty cakes (h).

Why pile them up? Bridge two cakes with a third for an unusual display (i).

Left: Violets and ribbons decorate this very pretty cake. Note that this clover-shaped cake has smooth icing with a delicate frill and that there is a basket of sugared almonds in lieu of individual gifts of favours.

Above: A croquembouche. The idea is French and truly delicious. Your own home-made choux pastry balls piled high in dishes, drenched in toffee or chocolate dessert sauce are a simpler-to-make alternative.

An explosion of colour, sight and sound to celebrate the big event.

Fireworks

Another way to add life, interest, colour and sound to your wedding celebrations is to use fireworks. Why not have a firework display as the highlight of your party or as a spectacular send-off for the bride and groom?

I'm not thinking of sparklers, bangers and roman candles here, but stunning and exciting displays: something to reflect the mood and style of your wedding. Options (and therefore prices) range from the sublime to the ridiculous and include small DIY packages, where you are in charge, right up to full-scale professionally orchestrated displays.

Firework displays can be stunning in the daytime, especially if you choose one of the 'parachute' packages: this is where an exploding rocket hurls hundreds of tiny multi-coloured parachutes into the air and these come floating down all around!

You may not believe it but you can use fireworks to reflect your particular wedding style. You could have a bright and noisy display at your up-beat disco party whilst another bride will choose a quiet and graceful colour-themed display to entertain her guests at a quiet country inn.

You don't have to seek formal permission to have a firework display, but it is important to inform local residents, as well as the local emergency services, who might otherwise be alarmed. You really do not want the local fire brigade adding extra excitement by turning up with blue lights flashing and hoses at the ready! Another thing to bear in mind is the time of day. There are no rules to say you can't have a display at midnight, but the locals may object. You don't want a nasty argument with outraged neighbours to spoil your party.

You shouldn't need to worry about special insurance against accidents, as your contract with the organising company should cover this. Check that it does. Satisfy yourself that the company you are dealing with offers a safe and professional service. If you intend to mount your own show, make sure a *responsible* adult is in complete charge and cognisant of the possible and very real dangers. Fireworks are not foolproof, so don't let a fool get near them to cause havoc at the end of your perfect day.

Gifts

Shortly after you announce that you are getting married, people will pester you about wedding presents. You will have to give some thought to this. Each family has its own little ways of organising this and you can choose how you wish to handle it: you can decline to receive any gifts at all; you can opt for donations to a favourite charity; you can open an account at a store and invite guests to contribute to a set of crockery or cutlery; you can write gifts on tear-out pages of a note book for circulation; or simply issue a list and accept what comes.

These days, many couples are already independent of their parents and both have their own homes and possessions. This means that when you get married you immediately have two of everything. When you add to this the wedding gifts, you could end up with three of everything!

On the face of it, it seems mercenary to send out a wedding gift list, but it is really the only way I know to stop people wasting their money on gifts that are not required.

If you do circulate a gift list, please stress that the buying of gifts is not mandatory. If you do think that giving gifts is compulsory, why don't you just sell tickets?

Exercise thought when you plan your list. It's nice to list things that are non-essentials. In this way you get to keep them longer, since things that are used infrequently don't get worn out so quickly. List things you'd never buy for yourself but long for (this does not include a Ferrari for himself or a new wardrobe for you!). Some of my favourite wedding gifts were crystal vases, a dinner service, picture frames and wine racks.

Other presents that were a joy to receive were those things you need but are really rather dull to have to buy: a spade and fork, bath towels, lampshades, rakes, shears, saucepans and place mats. Include plenty of lower priced items to ensure that guests have a reasonable choice.

Indicate colours where possible and it may be that you can include something of your wedding theme in your choice of gifts: all glass gifts, all crockery, all gardening items, all 'Country Diary', all 'Willow Pattern', all pinks, all 1950s, and so on.

Take time to check who is buying what and add the information straight away to a copy of the guest list and, later, make a further note of what they did buy. You'll need this to write thank-you letters. Don't assume you will remember everything and risk leaving someone out. You'll have enough to tax your memory as it is.

Yes, you must write or telephone your thanks. Don't use horrid pre-printed 'thank you' notes. Really show you are grateful, and do it as soon as possible. The honeymoon is an ideal time. What better way to occupy yourself as you lounge by the pool? And who says you can't write a thank-you note on a picture postcard from Majorca or San Francisco!

Photographs and Videos

Pick your photographer or video company with the greatest care. The photographs are the lasting items of your day and if they are dreadful you'll always regret it.

Initially I didn't want a video, but let my husband talk me into it. In the end I was delighted for I have since seen bits of my wedding that a bride never otherwise gets to see! I saw my groom and his best man waiting nervously outside the church. I saw them waiting for me in the front pew, and I saw all the faces of the guests in the church. A bride usually only sees the backs of people's heads as she walks up the aisle. Also, it's nice for the groom to see all the preparations that go on before the bride leaves the house. But better than all that for me, is that I can still hear my wedding. It's a wonderful memento and gets watched by sentimental relatives (and me) whenever the anniversary comes round.

Picking a video company also helped us to choose our photographer. We watched a number of sample videos (this is imperative to see that they know what they're doing) and as we watched I realised I was seeing a lot of footage of photographers. There seemed to be two main types: flash young things that whistled through it on a timetable ordering people about hither and yon, and then there were the slow old gentlemen that manhandled the bride into exact positions. I realised that I wouldn't tolerate either of these extremes, so I picked mine with care.

Having a photograph taken is nerve-racking at the best of times. On your wedding day, you can

It may be that your church or register office does not have very pleasant surroundings. Suggest local parks or stately homes to your photographer as alternatives, so he can capture you in a romantic setting. Don't forget that if the weather is dreadful, you can make arrangements to have some special photos taken after the honeymoon.

do without being aggravated or scared by the photographer. Choose someone you're happy to have pointing a camera at you.

How can you tell? Meet him beforehand. A good photographer will be happy to show you samples of his work if you ask. If he won't, don't use him. Also, if you approach a 'total service' agency and they can't guarantee who will take your photos, and if you can't check the quality to be expected, don't use them.

Ask your vicar if he has a favourite photographer; there may be a particular photographer he likes and would be happy for that particular professional to take photographs at certain times during the ceremony.

The same considerations are true of the video photographers. Meet them and decide if you want these people hanging around you on your special day. This is important since you don't want to be seen scowling at the camera because you don't like the cameraman!

With both the stills photographer and the video company, get the vicar's permission for them to work inside the church. Ask them if they know the church in question and send them there to check on the lighting conditions if they don't. A professional shouldn't need to be told.

Have a chat with them and see what special 'tricks' they can do for you. Videos can overlay your choice of music or the sound of bells (useful if you chose not to have them or if the church doesn't have any) and photographers can be imaginative in their use of double exposures and misty filters.

In Britain there is always a 50:50 chance that the weather will be rotten, so discuss the possibility of alternative indoor sets for the photographs. Also, if you live in a particularly beautiful area of the country, why not arrange a special photographic 'shoot' at one or some of the more notable beauty spots in the area? I know of a photographer in the Lake District who often takes a second set of photos after the wedding. He takes the most romantic set shots of the bride and groom at beauty spots like Ashness Bridge or on the edge of Lake Windemere.

Keepsakes

You are so busy being a bride and you are surrounded by so much love and attention that it is often hard to pause and take it all in. It is doubly hard to remember when the days and weeks pass. For this reason I would urge every bride to keep mementos and records of the day. The care and attention you and your family have put into making this the most special of days deserves to be preserved, admired and enjoyed again in the years to come.

Photographs or videos are one way of keeping memories. A look through bridal literature will show you many companies that specialise in other keepsakes: preserving bouquets, drying flowers, setting flowers in perspex, or setting photographs into china plates.

There are very many ways of keeping your memories, but surely the best are those you do yourself and I think all brides should consider at least one way of preserving something from their wedding.

Buy a little flower press especially for the occasion (good craft shops sell them) and press petals and leaves from your bouquet. When dry, arrange them into a picture and get hubby to use his nice new carpenter's kit to make you a frame.

Take a good close-up photograph of your bouquet and copy this for embroidery or tapestry for cushion covers. You can even knit it into a jumper if you wish.

If you have dried or silk flowers, pop them under a glass dome (possibly a cheese dome?) or get hubby to make you a glass case. Then again, why not dismantle the bouquet and make your own arrangement to put somewhere in pride of place.

Take ribbons from your bouquet or hair and keep them to sew into the christening gown for your future children.

Go to a craft shop and look at all the kits available that might be of use. For example, buy a kit to set mementoes of your wedding cake into perspex. No, I don't mean cake crumbs, but decorations or trimmings can make a nice show.

Save pieces of every type of wrapping paper. Cut it into small pieces and use it to cover a photoframe or a box for all your wedding trinkets.

Make a wedding cuttings book or buy one made especially for the purpose.

Use material from your gown to make a spectacular quilt or flouncy cushions for your bed. Of course, you may wish to keep your fabulous gown for use by other members of your family and if you do so, you will want to take special care of it.

A ring cushion made from cloth left over from making the wedding dress. If you can't bear the thought of anyone else wearing your dress, why not use it to make similar lacy and flouncy cushions and pile them up in romantic heaps on the bed.

Gifts made for a cat-lover. This handsome lucky black cat with his bride were a fun gift. The wedding colour was peach and so they are trimmed accordingly.

Storing your Dress

Whether you have worn a brand new dress or one that is already a family heirloom, the chances are that you will wish to store it for possible further use. With a little care there is no reason why your dress should not be kept in safe storage for many years.

Have the dress cleaned by professional cleaners as soon as possible after the wedding. Point out any areas that may have had things spilled on

Every bride gathers mementos; this bride boasts several hand-made gifts which are treasured. The lace trimmed horseshoe was made by a self-professed non-sewer. The effort that went into it made it all the more special.

them. Even though the stain may be invisible now, it could generate into a horrible blotch while in storage. If there are any dress shields in the gown, these should be removed and thrown away. If you are storing the hooped petticoat, remove the 'hoop' – especially if it is metal as it will discolour the fabric.

When clean, your dress should be wrapped in acid-free white paper to protect against creases. Put wadges of paper into the folds so that you 'bend' the dress rather than creating knife-edge creases. Puff up the tops of sleeves, etc. with paper. The dress should then be packed in a box which is in turn wrapped in plastic (to guard against moisture) and then placed in a large cardboard box which keeps out the light. Store it in a cool, dry place. This generally excludes the attic and the basement which can range through extremes of temperature and humidity depending on the time of year and weather. The wardrobe in the spare room is usually the favourite place.

After a year or so, and regularly thereafter, take it out to check for stains that may make a slow appearance. Return it to the cleaners if you find any. Re-wrap it just as carefully and put it away.

Wedding Day Worries

Talk to anyone who has been involved in organising a wedding and they will, without doubt, be able to regale you with tales of what went wrong, or nearly wrong. Nightmares and narrowly averted disasters may be the sort of thing that get a good laugh in the office, but they are the stuff of bride's nightmares.

It was some time after my wedding that my mother-in-law dared to tell me of her near disaster with our wedding cake. Whilst manoeuvring the very heavy cake to and from her gas oven, the greaseproof and brown-paper wrapping touched a flame and poor Joan was left with ten pounds of flaming cake in her arms! Although rescued unharmed by her husband, Joan nevertheless suffered agonies of worry until the wedding as she wondered whether we would notice the scorched taste! We didn't; it was the most delicious cake I've ever eaten.

Many years ago, during the week before my brother's wedding there was such a series of disasters that we wondered if it was worth the effort of planning a wedding that didn't want to happen! Amongst a whole catalogue of worries, we weathered pubs with no beer, the cat peeing on the bridesmaids' dresses and my brother losing his false teeth two days before the wedding! It was a week of horrors, and as the family council sat around bemoaning the fact that 'surely nothing else could go wrong' . . . a bag and a half of soot fell down the chimney! Even though the poor bride didn't know, until she reached the church, whether her groom would have any teeth, it had a happy end, for there is not a single miserable face in the wedding photographs. This was achieved by the simple expedient of telling the photographer to say 'teeth' instead of 'cheese'. He thought we were mad. Happy . . . but mad!

Insuring Yourselves Against the Worst

It may or may not be news to you that you can insure against some wedding disasters. Indeed, if you are spending a fortune or have incurred heavy loans to mount a special event it may well be worth paying a little extra to protect yourself from having it all wasted through accident or illness. Many insurance brokers can put together a wedding day package that is tailor-made to your needs. There are, however, standard wedding packages to cover the average wedding. Such policies generally cover the following: cancellation of the wedding through illness of bride, groom or relative; cancellation due to death, jury service, loss of job or being posted abroad; non-appearance of the photographer or damage to the negatives, so you have to retake photographs; damage to the wedding dress, suits or wedding presents; death or injury of someone at the wedding due to your negligence.

One thing an insurance company won't cover is good old-fashioned jilting. If either the bride or groom fail to turn up, that is just bad luck and poor judgement. Surprisingly it may be possible to insure against bad weather: so called 'pluvius' cover deals with this.

It's essential to read the small print to check exactly what is and is not covered, but in general one clause you are bound to find is one stating that you are expected to pay the first £25 or so of any claim. Check also your house contents policy: you may be pleasantly surprised to find it automatically increases the amount insured to cover loss or damage of wedding presents for a specified time up to and after the wedding – good news if you have generous friends and relatives and the house is stuffed with goodies.

Still, even if things do go wrong on the day it won't be an omen for the future. When Ruby and

Cyril Moore married in 1935 they had a few problems to contend with but nothing that really marred their day. However, they had a few superstitious qualms when they discovered their new house was to be number 13 and that it had 13 stairs. When their rather fine wedding present of a mantlepiece clock chimed 13 instead of one o'clock they had to wonder if luck was against the marriage. But 57 years later they're still going strong (and so is the clock!).

The Unique Bride

Ask anyone who has been married and they will tell you that it's not all roses. That is true of the wedding itself too. There are weeks and months of planning involved in preparing for a wedding. It is not necessarily all enjoyable, but does have to be done. Accept that there is as much labour as love in a wedding and you won't be disappointed or dismayed by all the hard work.

Do what you can to make your wedding a pleasure for you. Plan to do things, or have things happen that please you. Try and incorporate sentiment, family history and humour into your wedding plans and I am certain that you will find much more enjoyment in it all. That is the key. Your wedding is a celebration of the marriage between you and the man you love, make sure you enjoy it.

Whether you choose to commit yourself to a full-scale formal wedding, or whether you slip away quietly by yourselves and tell everyone about it afterwards, make sure that a marriage begun in that fashion is what you really want.

Many other men and women will marry on the same day as you: up and down the country, hundreds of other brides will flutter and worry and laugh and cry. I hope that this book has shown you that it is possible to make your wedding day special to you so that you can enjoy it with greater pleasure. Make sure that your wedding makes you happy and your wedding will stand out from all the many others on that day. You and your groom aren't just another couple on a sheet of statistics, your marriage is special; you are unique.

If you give thought now to the planning and preparation for your wedding, when you look back over the day, you'll have nothing but good things to remember.

Chapter 8

Inspiration and Ideas

This book has never been a pretender to the title of 'Wedding Planner' or 'Wedding Organiser', but one can't just leap into planning a wedding without some idea of the 'rules and regulations' so I have included some guidelines and checklists as a starting point.

There are many interesting and thorough books and planners on the market that you should invest in to make life easier, and don't forget that your local library is a useful resource. But don't just go to the etiquette and cake decorating sections: start with the oversize Royal books for full colour pageantry then move on to the history, biography, art and humour sections for inspiration.

This chapter is meant as a compilation of thoughts, ideas, designs and guides that you can use as a springboard for your own creativity. Almost every page has a border or motif that is there for you to copy, amend or improve. Whether you reproduce it in ink, in icing or embroidery is entirely up to you!

Wedding Planner

Assuming that you have found a man, worn him down and brought him to a proposal, the time is ripe to start planning. There are a lot of things to do. This list overleaf, although not definitive, is a start. If the service you require is popular or the wedding is in mid-summer, items marked * may need to be organised earlier.

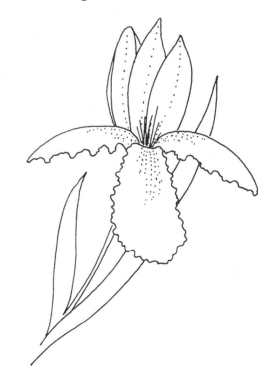

The Big Day

Enjoy yourself!

The Day Before

Finish packing
Final check of flowers and cake
Take going away clothes to hotel
Give best man money for fees and tips
Have an early night!

10 Days Before

Final fitting of wedding dress
Make wedding day appointment with hairdresser
Practise make up
Wear wedding shoes around house
Have rehearsal
Give Order of Service sheets to minister
Finalise arrangements with best man, bridesmaids
and ushers

Four Weeks Before

Chase up late replies to invitations
Confirm menus and numbers with caterers
Write place cards
Organise seating plan
Make hairdressing appointments
Confirm total numbers of buttonholes etc.
with florist

Confirm details with photographer
Confirm car hire
Notify bank and others of change of name
and address
Choose music and hymns
Discuss Order of Service cards with printer
and place order
Confirm travel and hotel bookings

Four Months Before

Confirm church arrangements and calling of banns
Book register office
Book hotel for wedding night
Visit doctor or family planning clinic
Buy wedding shoes, headdress, etc
Buy attendants' outfits
Arrange clothes for groom and others
Send invitations
Choose wedding rings and gifts for attendants

Six Months Before

Order invitations
Choose wedding dress (buy or hire)*
Organise wedding cake
Compile wedding present list
Book cars*
Book video*
Book photographer*
Arrange hire of tables, chairs, crockery or glasses if necessary
Apply for passports
Order flowers
Order stationery, souvenir cake-boxes, etc.

Nine to Twelve Months Before

Decide date, time and place
See minister, priest, rabbi or registrar and book ceremony*
Discuss budget
Book reception venue and caterers*
Decide on number of guests
Make guest list
Make honeymoon reservations*
Choose attendants and best man
Book dressmaker*
Book music and entertainment*

The Gift List

As I suggested in Chapter 7, you will find yourself besieged by friends who want to know what you would like as a wedding gift. Here is a list you might find useful.

Remember that you don't have to ask for everything on it! Be selective and perhaps limit yourself to requesting only one type of item: things for the kitchen, things for the dining table, things for the bedroom etc. That way, when you are married you can have one area absolutely complete. How wonderful it would be to invite friends to dinner and be able to serve them with perfectly matching, beautifully co-ordinated gifts.

For the Bedroom

Blankets	Duvets	Sheets
Pillowcases	Duvet covers	Valances
Dressing table set	Brush and comb set	Electric blanket
Bedside lamps	Reading lamps	Bedside clock
Hot water bottles	Tea maker	Clock radio alarm

For the Garden

Shears	Clothesline	Garden hand tools
Lawn edging tools	Lawn mower	
Bird boxes	Birdbath	Garden barrow
Bulbs	Hedge cutter	Shrubs
Grass rake	Fork and spade	Rake
Patio pots	Garden hose and reel	Patio furniture
		Watering can

For the Kitchen

Coffee maker	Food processor	Kettle
Cooker	Iron	Can opener
Refrigerator	Toaster	Cake tins
Bread bin	Bread board and knife	Casseroles
Storage tins		Corkscrew
Chopping board	Carpet sweeper	Floor mop
	Colander	Frying pan
Dustpan and brush	Egg whisk	Ironing board
	Flour sifter	Kitchen tools and rack
Flour bin	Grater	
Food mixer	Kitchen scissors	Mixing bowls
Kitchen knives		Rolling pin
Knife sharpener	Mincer	Slow cooker
	Pastry board	Scales
Omelette pan	Pressure cooker	Storage jars
Pepper mill	Microwave oven	Vegetable racks
Biscuit barrel		
Saucepans	Sieve	Wooden spoons
Strainers	Trays	
Washing-up bowl etc.	Waste bin	Spice rack
	Wok	
Food slicer	Tea cloths	

For the Living Room

Clock	Cushions	Occasional
Needlework	Nest of tables	table
basket	Standard lamp	Music centre
Radio	Bookshelves	Photo frames
Television set	Mirrors	

For the Bathroom

Bathroom	Bathroom	Indoor clothes
cabinets	scales	line
Pedal bin	Medicine	Towel Racks
Bath sheets	cabinet	Hand towels
Guest towels	Bath towels	Bath mat set
Bathrobe	Facecloths	Airer
Linen basket	Mirrors	

Cutlery

Table knives	Table forks	Dessert knives
Dessert forks	Dessert spoons	Fish knives
Fish servers	Cake knife	and forks
Soup spoons	Table spoons	Carving set
Coffee spoons	Grapefruit	Teaspoons
	knife	

Glass

Water jug	Champagne	Brandy glasses
Wine glasses	flutes	Liqueur glasses
Sherry glasses	Cocktail	Decanters
Sundae dishes	glasses	Salad bowls
Tumblers	Whisky glasses	Trifle bowls

For the Dining Room

Dinner service	Tea service	Candelabra
Cups and	Soup bowls	Breakfast set
saucers	Coffee pot	Sugar basin
Butter dish	Jugs	Coffee set
Fruit bowl	Condiment	Teapot
Milk jug	set	Table mats
Tablecloths	Tray cloths	Napkins
Napkin rings	Salad servers	Serving spoons
Toast rack	Tea strainer	Candlesticks

Miscellaneous

Vacuum	Pictures	Ice bucket
cleaner	Hostess trolley	Wine rack
Tea trolley	Tool box	Barbecue
Power tools		

Bridal Fabrics

Brocade Heavy fabric with woven raised design, often with matt and shiny pattern.

Chiffon Thin gauzy fabric, often silk or rayon, with either a soft and floaty or crisp finish.

Chintz Cotton fabric (sometimes glazed) printed with floral designs.

Moiré Silk taffeta patterned to shine like water when illuminated.

Muslin Cotton gauze cloth, almost transparent.

Organdie Sheer, crisply textured fabric, almost transparent.

Satin Silky fabric with glossy surface on one side.

Shantung Rough-textured plain weave silk or man-made fibre.

Taffeta Crisp smooth fabric with small crosswise rib.

Tulle Fine, sheer net fabric of silk, nylon or rayon.

Bridesmaids' Dresses Measurement Chart

	1	2	3	4
Name				
Age				
A Chest/Bust				
B Waist				
C Hips				
D Back of neck to waist				
E Width of shoulders				
F Length underarm seam				
G Length outside arm seam				
H Thickness upper arm				
I Thickness wrist				
J Depth of waist to hip				
K Back of neck to floor/hem				
L Waist to floor/hem				
M Floor to hem				
N Around neck				

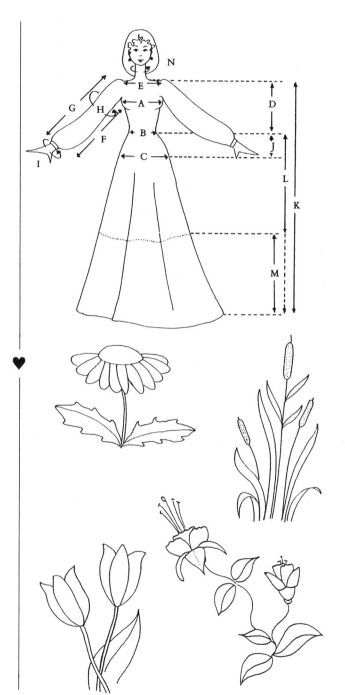

Wedding Dress Measurement Chart

		cm	in
A	Bust		
B	Waist		
C	Hips		
D	Back of neck to waist		
E	Width of shoulders		
F	Length underarm seam		
G	Length outside arm seam		
H	Thickness upper arm		
I	Thickness wrist		
J	Depth of waist to hip		
K	Back of neck to floor/hem		
L	Waist to floor/hem		
M	Floor to hem		
N	Around neck		

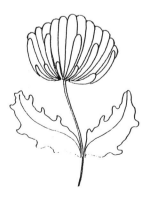

Signs of the Zodiac

As I suggested in Chapter 1, there are many items and legends associated with the date of our birth. Here is a list of all sorts of items associated with signs of the zodiac, stars, planets and birthdays. If you haven't a clue what colour to pick as a theme and you're born under the sign of Taurus the bull, then you can pick yellow and when everyone asks why, you can simply say 'It's lucky for me . . .'

Aries
21 Mar-20 Apr

The ram was a hero who was sent to rescue two children. When it died, its fleece (of gold) was hung in a sacred grove and it was honoured in the sky. This was the golden fleece for which the Argonauts searched.

Planet:	Mars
Colours:	red, scarlet
Metals:	iron, steel
Stones:	jasper, malachite, diamond
Number:	3
Animal:	dog

Taurus
21 Apr-21 May

Jupiter fell in love with Europa and decided to abduct her. He took the shape of a white bull, coaxed her to ride him then dashed off into the sea with her!

Planet:	Venus
Colours:	yellow, pale blue, all pastels
Metals:	copper, brass
Stones:	lapis-lazuli, carnelian
Number:	6
Animal:	cock

Gemini
22 May-21 Jun

Although twins, Pollux was immortal whilst Castor was not. When Castor was killed, Pollux wished to share his immortality with his brother. Jupiter placed them both in the sky.

Planet:	Mercury
Colours:	blue, violet
Metals:	mercury
Stones:	agate, topaz,
Number:	4
Animal:	ape

Cancer
22 Jun-22 Jul

The crab represents a giant sea crab which appeared to help the Hydra when it was doing battle with Hercules. Hercules crushed the crab underfoot and Juno placed it in the sky.

Planet:	Moon
Colours:	green, white, silver
Metals:	silver, aluminium
Stones:	emerald, crystal, pearl
Number:	2
Animal:	ram

Leo
23 Jul-23 Aug

Leo was another of the great mythical beasts that the hero Hercules slayed. The lion was placed in the heavens by a goddess who was displeased with Hercules.

Planet:	Sun
Colours:	orange, gold, yellow
Metals:	gold
Stones:	ruby
Number:	1
Animal:	horse

Virgo
24 Aug-23 Sep

The virgo represents the goddess Astraea who became so disgusted with Mankind that she retired to the heavens.

Planet:	Mercury
Colours:	blue, violet
Metals:	mercury
Stones:	agate, topaz
Number:	4
Animal:	snake

Libra
24 Sep-23 Oct

In Greek legend the scales commemorate Mochis the inventor of weights and measures.

Planet:	Venus
Colours:	yellow, pale blue, all pastels
Metals:	copper, brass
Stones:	lapis-lazuli, carnelian
Number:	6
Animal:	dragon

Scorpio
24 Oct-22 Nov

In mythology the scorpion arose from the ground to attack the great hunter Orion.

Planet:	Mars
Colours:	red, scarlet
Metals:	iron, steel
Stones:	jasper, malachite, diamond
Number:	3
Animal:	hare

Sagittarius
23 Nov-21 Dec

This represents the centaur that was tutor to Jason and Hercules and who also was a guide to Jason in the quest for the golden fleece.

Planet:	Jupiter
Colours:	violet, purple
Metals:	tin
Stones:	amethyst, moonstone
Number:	5
Animal:	tiger

Capricorn
22 Dec-20 Jan

The sea goat is associated with the demi-god Pan and thus all shepherds and pastoral life.

Planet:	Neptune
Colours:	mauve, lavender, blood-red
Metals:	platinum
Stones:	ivory
Number:	9
Animal:	pig

Aquarius
21 Jan-19 Feb

The water carrier represents Ganymede, a cupbearer of the Gods.

Planet:	Uranus
Colours:	azure, electric-tones
Metals:	uranium, radium
Stones:	amber
Number:	8
Animal:	rat

Pisces
20 Feb-20 Mar

Venus and Cupid escaped from the giant Typhon by leaping into the River Euphrates as fish.

Planet:	Saturn
Colours:	indigo, grey, black
Metals:	lead
Stones:	sapphire, jet, onyx
Number:	7
Animal:	bull

Civil and Religious Authorities

If you require information about marrying outside your own church, your local parish or even the country, then the following organisations may be of help to you.

Church of England Enquiry Centre, Church House, Dean's Yard, London, SW1P 3NZ (071 222 9011).

Catholic Marriage Advisory Council, Clitheroe House, 1 Blythe Mews, Blythe Road, London W14 0NW (071 371 1341).

Baptist Union, Baptist House, 129 Broadway, Didcot OX11 8RT (0235 512077).

Jewish Marriage Council, 23 Ravenhurst Avenue, London NW4 4EE (081 203 6311) (marriage preparation courses).

Marriage Authorisation Office, Office of Chief Rabbi, Adler House, Tavistock Square, London WC1 (071 387 1066) (religious queries).

United Reform Church, 86 Tavistock Place, London WC1H 9RT (071 837 7661).

Registrar of the Province of Canterbury, 1 The Sanctuary, London SW1 (071 222 5381).

General Register Office for Scotland, New Register House, Edinburgh EH1 3YT (031 334 0380).

General Register Office, Oxford House, 49-55 Chichester Street, Belfast BT1 4HL (0232 235211).

The Registrar General, Custom House, Dublin 17 (Eire).

Methodist Press Service, 1 Central Buildings, Westminster, London SW1 (071 222 8010).

Church of Scotland, 121 George Street, Edinburgh EH2 4YN (031 225 5722).

Image Bank

Image Bank

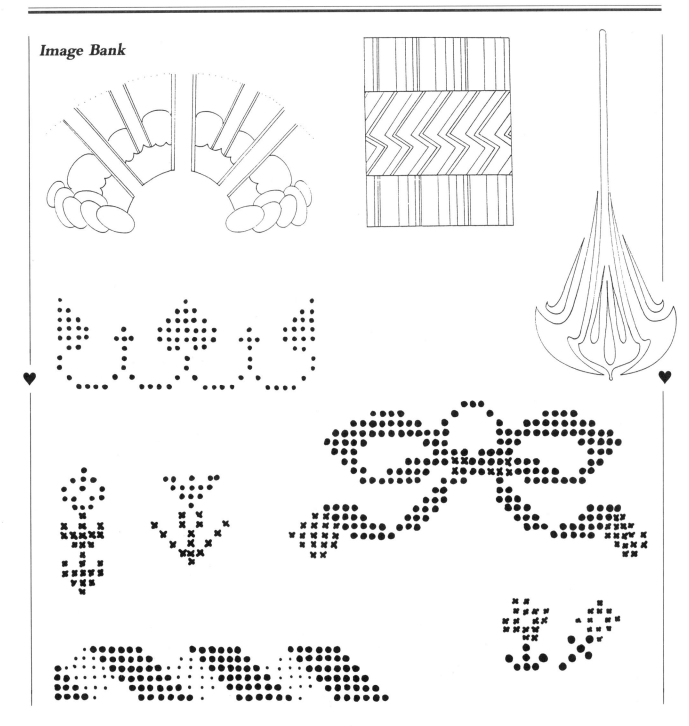

Image Bank — Needlecraft

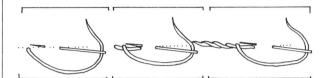

Stem stitch.

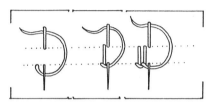

Buttonhole stitch.

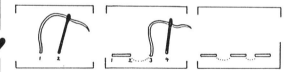

Running stitch.

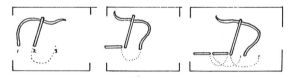

Back stitch.

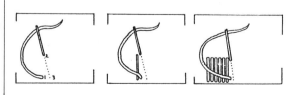

Satin stitch.

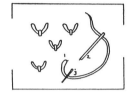

Fly/feather stitch.

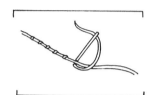

Couching.

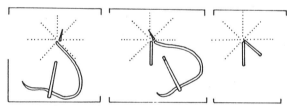

Straight daisy stitch.

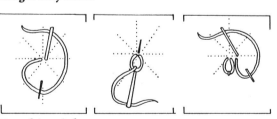

Lazy daisy stitch.

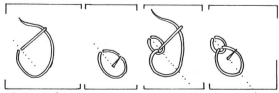

Chain stitch.

Bibliography

The Art of Origami, Paper Folding Traditional and Modern, Samuel Randlett, Faber & Faber, 1963, ISBN 0 571 663527.

The Art of Sugar Craft: Royal Icing, Brenda Purton, Merehurst Press, ISBN 0 948075 538.

Honiton Lace Patterns, Elsie Luxton, B.T. Batsford Ltd, 1983, ISBN 0 7134 4135 6.

Paper Folding Fun, Origami in Colour, Zulal Aytura-Scheele, Octopus Books, 1986, ISBN 0 7064 26193.

French Style – Embroidery, Conran, Octopus Books, 1986, ISBN 1 85029 0466.

Creative Caligraphy, Marie Lynskey, Thorsons Publishers Ltd, 1988, ISBN 0 7225 1509X.

Wedding Bouquets, Mary Gudgeon & John Clowes, M&J Publications Ltd, 1987, ISBN 0 9509748 2X.

Wedding Flowers, Pauline Mann, B.T. Batsford Ltd, 1985, ISBN 0 7134 4636 6.

BRIDES Book of Etiquette, Editors of BRIDES magazine, Perigee Books, 1989, ISBN 0 399 5501 1.

Brides, A Complete Guide to Your Wedding, BRIDES and Setting Up Home magazine, Peerage Books, 1988, ISBN 1 85052 104 2.

The Creative Book of Table Decorations, Susie Smith & Karen Lansdown, Salamander Books, 1987, ISBN 0 86101 2917.

The Encyclopedia of World Costume, Doreen Yarwood, B.T. Batsford Ltd, 1988, ISBN 0 7134 1340 9.

Pamela Peake's Catcraft, Guild Publishing (Book Club Assoc and William Collins & Sons), 1984.

Make Your Own Gloves, Gwen Emlyn-Jones, G. Bell & Sons, 1974, ISBN 0 7135 17735.

GOOD HOUSEKEEPING Crochet Designs, Ebury Press, Dorling Kindersley, 1984, ISBN 0 85223 3183.

Embroidery with Beads, Angela Thompson, B.T. Batsford Ltd, 1987, ISBN 0 7134 5495 4.

The Illustrated Encyclopaedia of Costume and Fashion, Jack Cassin Scott, Blandford Press, 1986, ISBN 0 7137 1811 0.

The Country Diary of an Edwardian Lady, Edith Holden, Webb & Bower Ltd/Michael Joseph Ltd, 1977, ISBN 07181 15813.

The Observer's Book of Astronomy, Patrick Moore, Frederick Warner & Co Ltd, 1971, ISBN 0 7232 00939.

Suppliers and Services

I would like to acknowledge the time and help given to me by the following individuals and companies. Some of these companies may not supply direct to the general public but will be able to give you details of retail outlets.

Wykraft Products (Bead Suppliers), 8 Tarrant Way, Moulton, Northampton NN3 1US. (0604 44889)

Moss Bros Group Plc, 8 St John's Hill, London SW11 1SA.   (071 924 1717)

Randall Williams Photography (Chris Titmus), 94 Broadwater Crescent, Stevenage, Herts SG2 8EE.   (0438 355420)

The Food and Photography Co. (Jeff and Cally Rand), The Studio, Bumper Hall Penn, Royston Road, Littlington, Herts SG8 0RL. (0763 853170)

Kirgloves Hitchin Ltd, Bury Mead Road, Hitchin, Herts SG5 1RU.   (0462 432392)

Iris Martin Lace Making Supplies, Farthing Cottage, Chickens Yard, Yardley Road, Olney, Beds.   (0234 712446)

Romance Unlimited, Rita Williamson, 20 Lynton Avenue, Arlesey, Beds SG15 6TT.   (0462 732566)

Fantastic Fireworks Ltd, Rocket House, Redbourn, Herts AL3 7RH.   (0582 485544)

Dropinstitches (Knitting), 3 Bedwell Park, Bedwell Crescent, Stevenage, Herts SG1 1NB. (0438 725155)

CVR Cars, 2 Lonsdale Road, Stevenage, Herts SG1 5ES.   (0438 357879)

Heli-flair Ltd (Helicopter Hire), Goodwood Airfield, Chichester, West Sussex PO18 0PH. (0243 779222)

BOC Ltd, The Priestly Centre, 10 Priestly Road, Surrey Research Park, Guildford, Surrey GU2 5XY.   (Balloon Hotline 0483 579857)

Jackie Marklew (Zandra Rhodes Collection), Jones and Brother, Shepley Street, Guide Bridge, Audenshaw, Manchester M34 5JD. (061 330 6531).

Linda MacDonald, Butterick Company Limited, New Lane, Havant, Hants PO9 2ND. (0705 486221)

The Wedding Association, 60-62 Kings Road, Reading, Berks.   (0734 509345)

Meadowbrook Design (preserving bouquets), Kibworth Beauchamp, Leicestershire LE8 0HW. (0533 792923)

Berkertex Ltd, Precedent Drive, Rooksley, Milton Keynes MK13 8PL.   (0908 669977)

John M. Walker, Photographer, The Wedding Bell. (071 474 9222)

Index

Figures in italics refer to captions.